REMEMBERING RUTH

REMEMBERING RUTH

A Memoir of Childhood Sibling Loss

Judy Eichinger

Full Court Press
Englewood Cliffs, New Jersey

First Edition

Copyright © 2018 by Judy Eichinger

Published in the United States of America
by Full Court Press, 601 Palisade Avenue,
Englewood Cliffs, NJ 07632
fullcourtpressnj.com

ISBN 978-1-946989-12-3
Library of Congress Catalog No. 2018935735

Some names in this book have been changed
for reasons of privacy.

Cover art by Bob Eichinger

*Editing and book design by Barry Sheinkopf for Bookshapers
(bookshapers.com)*

FOR ALL BEREAVED SIBLINGS

PROLOGUE

More than fifty years later, I still remember what happened immediately after my sister died. She was critically ill in the hospital, and my parents and I had been maintaining a vigil. Friends and relatives came and went. My parents rarely left her room, and I hung out in the waiting room down the hall, smoking menthol cigarettes—a habit I'd just begun to stem my nervousness.

My parents' good friend Abe stuck his head in the waiting room doorway. "Wanna go down to the cafeteria to get an ice cream soda?"

As we sipped our sodas, he made small talk. When we were finished, we went back upstairs. My father was standing outside my sister's room, tears streaming down his face. My mother was inside.

"She's gone," he said.

I felt numb with shock and disbelief. My parents—knowing that Ruth was about to die—had sent me away to protect me, but I couldn't forgive them. My mother and father had shared with Ruth her last moment of life and left me out. It was the ultimate betrayal.

Two nights before, Ruth had been rushed to the hospital, talking incoherently and slipping in and out of a coma. Earlier that evening I had gone out on a blind date. When I left, I had felt a certain foreboding. She had been sick many times before, but I was really scared this time. I'd held back tears all evening and couldn't wait for the date to end.

When I returned home, I had tiptoed into Ruth's room to join the family.

"What's happening?" I'd asked.

My mother had seemed frantic. "Go to bed," my dad said.

In my room I started having silent heaves. I was crying hysterically inside and praying that Ruth wouldn't die.

A few minutes later, one of my parents yelled to me, "Call an ambulance." I tried to dial the number—taped on the phone—but couldn't get my fingers and brain to work together. Mom ended up dialing for me.

I rode behind the ambulance in a neighbor's car and thought, This is it. In a short while, I will no longer have a sister. Two days later, Ruth was dead.

Before

CHAPTER 1

THERE WAS A POINT IN MY ADULT LIFE when I organized a six-week sibling-loss support group. There were four of us, led by a therapist whose mother had lost a brother during her childhood. She knew how much the loss had affected her mother's life, and she wanted to learn more about it. For this reason, she was willing to lead the support group without charging a fee.

During our third session, she gave us an assignment. "Write down all the good times you had with your brother or sister."

I tried to remember the good times when we were growing up and couldn't. So I spoke to my cousin Terri, because she and Ruth had been close in age. "Did you and Ruth have any fun together?"

"Oh, yes," she said. "Whenever I stayed at your house, we'd laugh hysterically at bed time as we jumped up and down on our beds. When we heard one of your parents coming up the stairs to check on what the ruckus was all about, we'd dive under the covers and pretend to be asleep."

Then it dawned on me. I couldn't remember the fun because, from an early age, I had always worried about her.

I was two and a half when Ruth was born. Not long after her birth, doctors discovered that one of her kidneys was completely shriveled; the other was severely damaged and barely functioning. As a result, her kidneys couldn't adequately filter body wastes, and she often got sick.

My first memory of her being sick was waiting in the car with my dad in New York City while Mom took Ruth to see a specialist. I didn't know what was going on, but the mood was somber. I was very young at the time.

My parents tried to maintain a semblance of normalcy as much as possible. Ruth went to school, and we'd go out to dinner and get together with other families. However, emergencies often occurred, especially at night.

Until I was eight, we lived in an apartment on Highland Boulevard in the East New York section of Brooklyn. Ruth and I slept in twin beds in the bedroom, and our parents used a convertible couch in the living room.

One night I woke up to gurgling noises. Ruth was sitting up in bed, vomiting blood. She was rushed to the hospital, where she stayed for several days. Children were not allowed to visit. Outside the building, Dad held me up, and Mom waved to me from the sixth-floor window. I waved back.

My sister was often admitted to the hospital. If there was time, I'd be dropped off at a relative's apartment. Once I remember staying with my great aunt Anna, whom I loved a lot. However, at one moment I was nervous and was biting my nails. "That's a bad habit, and you should stop," she warned me.

One summer day, our family visited a family at the Jersey shore. By this time, we had moved to Millburn, New Jersey. I went with Ruth and several other kids to the local amusement park. It was early evening and getting cool. Ruth and I decided to ride on the Ferris wheel. Soon after we lowered the safety bar, our swinging chair began to rise. When we reached the top, the Ferris wheel stopped.

We seemed to stay up there forever, and Ruth said, "I'm cold." She began shivering.

"Get us down, please!" I shouted to the people below, but they didn't hear me. I tried to keep her warm but couldn't. It seemed as if we had been stuck forever when suddenly we started moving again. As we circled around, I yelled that we wanted to get off. When we reached the bottom, the attendant stopped the wheel and let us off.

I have hated amusement parks ever since. I feel lonely and vulnerable whenever I go to one with my grandchildren. They love the rides, and I have to hide my feelings of terror and foreboding. It's always a relief when we leave.

When Ruth had a crisis, she was usually taken to Mountainside Hospital in Montclair. However, once when she was very sick, my parents took her to a specialist at New York Hospital in Manhattan, and I went along with them. The doctor said Ruth needed a transfusion. The resident who administered the transfusion gave it to her too quickly, and her pulse rate soared. She began breathing very rapidly, and there was a good chance she wouldn't survive the night.

It was late, and Dad and I went to the hotel across the street while Mom stayed with her. I tried to sleep, but it seemed impossible. I kept waiting for the phone to ring. Finally, I dozed off. I woke up in a panic. It was morning. Ruth had made it through the night and survived the latest crisis.

CHAPTER 2

OUSIN TERRI'S RECOLLECTION OF RUTH as fun-loving and spontaneous helped me remember that Ruth and I had shared lots of good times together. I'd buried those memories because it hurt so much to remember.

We'd been buddies and allies. We sided with each other, especially if either of us disagreed with something our parents did or said. At the round table tucked into the kitchen alcove where the four of us usually had dinner, Ruth or I would begin giggling about something, and the other would join in.

"What's so funny?" one of our parents would ask.

"Oh, nothing," we'd answer in near unison, and our giggling would increase in intensity.

We became co-conspirators each year before our parents' wedding anniversary. We always planned a surprise event. Once we made dinner for them and served it in the dining room. Included on the menu was prune whip, the first dessert Mom had made for Dad after they were married.

Another year, we arranged for dinner at a local restaurant, followed by a musical at the Paper Mill Playhouse. We set up a scavenger hunt for them to discover where they were going.

Ruth and I danced in the rain outside the Crandon Motor Court in Key Biscayne, Florida, played with the family dog in the back yard, and squeezed into the same miniature fire truck at an amusement park ride—though all the other fire engines were empty. Often we played "wedding," using one of our mom's robes as the bridal gown, and put on a number of original theatrical productions starring the two of us.

When Ruth wasn't being rushed to the hospital because she was coughing up blood, spiking a high temperature, or needing an emergency transfusion, she was like any other kid her age. She was a good student, though she often missed school. She was lots of fun and had lots of friends.

One of Ruth's classmates, beginning in kindergarten, was Lorre Wyatt, later a well-known musician in folk-singing circles who was Pete Seeger's long time friend and collaborator. Lorre was smitten with Ruth from the first time he met her when they were six years old and has lots of stories of her that he's told me.

He recalls how Ruth enjoyed nature walks with her elementary school class, even though her classmates made fun of the activity. "On one walk, Ruth became very excited when she spotted a scarlet tanager. She couldn't stop talking about it."

Lorre and Ruth sometimes strolled to Taylor Park, a block from our house. "I was throwing stones in the pond one day, and I asked Ruth how long she thought it would take for the ripples from her stone to reach the far side.

"'I don't think my ripples will reach the other side,' she replied."

Ruth told him how much she loved doing things with me as well. (I didn't know this.) Once he asked her to walk with him to Gruenings, a popular casual restaurant a couple of miles away, to get some ice cream. "I'm going there with Judy," she told him proudly.

She and I had our fights. We called each other names and participated in occasional screaming matches. Once I was so angry I ran upstairs after Ruth and threw my hairbrush at her. It hit her back, and my mother exploded. "Don't you know you could *kill* her if you hit her kidney?"

I was guilt-ridden and filled with remorse. It was true that a strong blow to Ruth's lower back could potentially be fatal. My mother's fear kindled my own, and I was relieved once I knew Ruth was okay.

At the same time, I was angry. Why couldn't we fight fair and square like other kids without my having to worry that my anger might kill?

When just such a damaging blow in fact happened in July 1959, it had nothing to do with me. Our family was spending part of the summer at the Hidden Valley Health Ranch in Escondido, California. My parents hoped Ruth would benefit from a special diet regimen. She was sitting on a horse, and an experienced trainer was leading them around the grounds. Suddenly, something made the horse buck, and she was thrown to the ground. Her health steadily deteriorated after the accident. She died nine months later.

CHAPTER 3

AVING A CHRONICALLY ILL YOUNGER SIBLING made me very independent at an early age. Often, my parents were busy with Ruth, and I made my own breakfast. (They bragged that I could cook hot oatmeal when I was five.) I went to sleep-away camp when I was six, although most camps didn't accept youngsters for overnight programs until they were older. That summer my parents were dealing with one of my sister's serious health crises, and a friend of theirs who ran a summer camp agreed to take me. I wasn't happy, because I missed my family. I don't remember much about that summer, but for one new skill I learned: how to blow bubbles with Bazooka bubble gum.

When I got older I went to Girl Scout camp, and that was a happier experience. I had been eight, and Ruth five, when we moved to Millburn. During each of the following two summers, I spent a week at camp in Essex County's South Mountain Reservation, about fifteen minutes from home. We lived in screened-in cabins and cooked campfire stew and tuna wiggle. The cabins circled a huge field where we played sports during the day and stargazed at night. There were periodic head checks for "nits," although I don't remember what the remedy was if you had them. It was fun, and I went with a number of kids from school.

At eleven, I began spending a month each summer at Eagle Island, another of the county's Girl Scout camps. It occupied an island in the middle of Upper Saranac Lake in New York State's Adirondack Mountains. It took eight hours by chartered bus to get there, but I thought it was heaven on earth. I spent six summers there, and when I was there I sometimes forgot about Ruth's latest health crisis.

Eagle Island became my salvation. I made friends with a group of girls who came from towns near my own, and we returned together year after year. Eagle Island remains dear to my heart to this day. I can still smell the pines and hear the ripple of the water along the shore. I was well liked and felt part of something bigger than myself. We slept in tents on platforms in the middle of the woods, and used outhouses. We walked down wooded paths to the showers, where, often, the water was cold. Yet the majestic trees and natural beauty captivated me.

I learned to swim at Eagle Island, although I never had the stamina to pass the lifeguard test. I learned how to row a boat, paddle a canoe, and man a sailboat. We played outdoor and indoor games, took hikes, and sat around the campfire, singing songs.

Often we met in the main lodge after dinner for an evening program. Afterward, we'd go out on the porch, wrap our arms around each others' waists, and sway as we sang our closing song, "Peace I Ask of Thee, O River," a standard from the Girl Scouts Fifties songbook:

Peace I ask of thee, O river,
Peace, peace, peace.
When I learn to live serenely
Cares will cease.

From the hills I gather courage,
Visions of the days to be,
Strength to lead and faith to follow
All are given unto me.

It was dark, and we could hear the rippling water, smell the pines, and feel the breezes. It *was* very serene. We'd follow that song by singing "Taps:"

Day is done, gone the sun, from the lake,
from the hills, from the sky;
all is well, safely rest,
God is nigh.

Then we'd say together,

God bless the Girl Scouts and Girl
Guides all over the world tonight.

And with only our flashlights for illumination, we'd wend our way up the narrow paths leading to our tents.

When I was fifteen, I joined the camp's Tripper unit, composed of ten girls and two counselors. We went on a three-day and then a ten-day canoe trip. We paddled through a chain of lakes in the

Adirondacks, portaging our canoes from one lake to the next. It was so beautiful, so quiet. Most of the sounds came from birds, faraway animals, and our paddles stroking the water. Each night we slept under the trees. If it rained, we wrapped tarps under and over ourselves and used the canoes as partial shelters. We made sure the food was securely packed and hung high enough on tree branches to be out of the reach of bears. There were no cell phones then. We were on our own, yet I don't remember ever worrying about my safety.

One thing I never talked about at camp was my sister's illness. My camp friends had no idea that she was so sick. Each summer, I buried that part of my life deep inside me.

At the time, I never knew how jealous Ruth was that I got to go to camp and she had to stay home. Mom told me much later that my sister was inconsolable after my bus left for camp. She wanted so much to go too, and couldn't.

Mom and Dad and Ruth would venture to Eagle Island on visiting day. Because it was such a long car ride there and back, they usually took a small plane. They couldn't land on the island, but there was an airport on the mainland not far from camp. Ruth was always very sad when she had to leave.

A week after her death, one of my camp buddies called. "I heard your sister was sick," she said. "How's she doing?"

"She died."

There was silence. The friend was stunned. She said how sorry she was, and we hung up. I never heard from her again.

CHAPTER 4

S UMMER CAMP PLAYED AN IMPORTANT ROLE in my parents'
life. They met as camp counselors. Mom was nineteen, Dad
eighteen. She'd been born outside Chicago, and ten years
old when her father left the family for another woman. Mom's
mother—my grandma Mary—was bitter and had a hard time raising three children on her own, isolated from her extended family,
so she moved to the Bronx to be near one of her sisters. Mom finished high school and worked in retail at B. Altman. She always
regretted that she hadn't been able to go to college. At the time,
she needed to work to help support the family.

Dad grew up in the Marine Park section of Brooklyn with his
parents, two brothers, and a sister. He was attending Brooklyn College when he met Mom.

In addition to his summer work as a camp counselor, he tutored
math and held other jobs to make his way through school. He went
on to Brooklyn Polytechnic Institute and graduated with a degree
in Engineering.

Mom and Dad saved for five years before getting married. By that time, she'd been employed for several years. Dad was teaching math and had begun working in his father's failing rubber stamp business to try to turn it around.

One thing was never in doubt: Mom and Dad were very much in love. They were both very attractive. She was a pretty brunette of medium height with a warm smile and wavy hair that fell just below her ears; he was several inches taller, had a muscular body from playing sports, a ready grin, and dark-brown hair parted in the middle. But the attraction was much more than skin deep. They cared deeply for each other and would be devoted soulmates until Dad died of colon cancer when he was fifty-seven—eleven years after Ruth died, and just months after I got married.

Passages in Mom and Dad's first years of their life together happened in five-year increments. They dated for five years, and five years after their marriage, I was born.

The pattern was broken when Ruth arrived two and a half years later. Our parents welcomed each of us with open arms and lots of love.

CHAPTER 5

I DIDN'T UNDERSTAND BEFORE RUTH DIED that I was often angry and jealous as well as sad and frightened—-angry because her illness often got in the way of some special event in which I was involved. At those times, I wanted my parents' undivided attention. Instead, her needs took precedence.

The All-State Chorus and Orchestra performed every year at the New Jersey Education Association Convention in Atlantic City. I auditioned for the first time in my junior year and was thrilled to be chosen.

A few days before the concert, I traveled there by bus with other high school participants from Northern New Jersey. My parents and Ruth planned to come down the day before the concert.

Singing with that prestigious group was unforgettable. Even the tryout gave me goose bumps. We had to sing the spiritual "A Balm in Gilead." I sang alto, with other contenders singing soprano, tenor, and bass. Listening to the blend of four voices sent shivers up my spine.

At the first rehearsal in Convention Hall, a vast auditorium with close to fifteen thousand seats, our chorus of two-hundred-plus high schoolers seemed very small when we rehearsed in the cavernous space. I looked around and realized there were no support columns, an engineering feat. The barrel vault ceiling consisted of aluminum tiles decorated to resemble Roman bath tiles. To one side sat a huge pipe organ. I found out later it was the largest musical instrument in the world, with over 33,000 pipes.

We warmed up by singing our audition piece. I welled up hearing the collective sound. Then we practiced *Carmina Burana*, a cantata composed by Carl Orff that was the centerpiece of the concert. I'd never heard it before, and I loved it.

The day after I got there, I called home. When Mom answered the phone, I could tell something was wrong.

"Ruth is sick, and we might not be able to come," she said. I didn't reply but felt heartbroken.

We spoke a couple of times later that day, and it seemed more doubtful that they would make it. But the following morning—the day of the performance—Mom said that Ruth had rallied and they were coming. They showed up just before the concert began. Afterwards, they said they had enjoyed it very much, but it was obvious they were preoccupied with my sister.

RUTH OFTEN GOT MORE ATTENTION than I did from some relatives when they greeted us. They'd hug her and cuddle her; I remained on the sideline. I knew my parents loved both of us, but it was invariably Ruth who always ended up in Dad's lap. Once I heard a relative comment, "Judy seems cold and unfeeling." These words stung deeply, but I didn't let my feelings show.

I was also angry that I had to be extra careful around Ruth, especially if we were arguing about something. I thought, *God forbid I should injure her.*

One incident remains seared on my mind. We were sitting at opposite ends of the living room couch, disagreeing about something. I had a sharpened pencil in my hand. We started arguing and things became more heated. Finally, I screamed and threw the pencil at her. The point penetrated the skin close to her right eye. It left a visible piece of graphite embedded just beneath the surface. Every time I looked at her, I remembered how close I'd come to damaging her vision.

Growing up I felt apart from other kids. I didn't talk about it or fully realize it at the time. I went around with a group of girls who liked me, and two considered me to be a close friend. But I didn't open up to them about my deepest feelings and longings, though one of them had a younger brother who was physically and mentally handicapped. Because of my reluctance to talk about Ruth and how worried I was about her, they were stunned when she died.

"You never revealed how sick Ruth was," one of them said. It was a secret I had kept inside behind a veneer of independence.

"Judy's been self-reliant and independent from an early age," my parents often told others. They were emotionally focused on Ruth and called that independence a virtue. For a long time, I felt proud of being able to take care of myself. But I paid a price by not getting close to anyone my own age.

CHAPTER 6

I DIDN'T ATTEND ANY OF MY HIGH SCHOOL REUNIONS until the fiftieth, and then I went to only one event. It took me a long time to figure out why. All through school there had been two Judys. One was the exterior Judy who had been voted Miss Versatile by her senior class. She played the flute, sang in the New Jersey All-State Chorus, was captain of the baton twirlers, and got elected class secretary.

The interior Judy was always sad inside, couldn't express her deepest feelings to friends, and often went to the basement to cry her eyes out because she was so afraid that her sister would die. The thought of going to a reunion brought back the deep pain she had felt during those years.

Still, there were many moments growing up, in addition to camp, that I cherish to this day. Some involved my family. For instance, whenever Dad said the word, "Meatball," I would crack up. I can't remember the original reference, but the word referred to a dog, not a food. Dad had told a funny story about a dog named

Meatball, and I had laughed hysterically. After that, whenever he wanted me to lose it, he'd say, "Meatball." It worked every time.

Mom was famous for her brown sauce. She was a good cook, and I enjoyed many of her signature dishes—sweet and sour tongue, sweet potato and apple casserole, shepherd's pie, and the best chicken matzoh ball soup in the world. (She claimed the secret to the soup's incredible flavor was the inclusion of chicken feet and lots of dill.) And once, when she was cooking string beans, she left them on the stove too long and burned them. I loved the taste, though, and thought the brown sauce was intentional. From then on, I always asked that she make them that way.

Our family was one of the last in our neighborhood to get a television. We listened to *The Lone Ranger* and *The Shadow* in front of a console radio in the living room. Dad and Mom sat on wing chairs, and Ruth and I sprawled out on our stomachs with our heads resting on our bent arms. When we finally got a TV, my parents put it on a low table in their bedroom. After dinner, Ruth and I would each bring a snack upstairs and sit on the edge of their beds (two twins pushed together) to watch. I loved graham crackers softened with milk the best.

Every year Millburn held a Halloween parade, and Dad made Ruth's and my costumes. They were very inventive, and we always took home the top prize. For example, one year Ruth was a flower pot and I was a watering can.

Before my father's parents died, we got together with Dad's family in Brooklyn and sometimes went to Lundy's for a shore dinner. I'd share steamed clams with Poppy, my dad's father. Dad's side of the family also liked to go fishing, and we sometimes went to the Jersey shore and rented a couple of outboard motorboats.

Every other winter, we visited Mom's relatives in Miami. My grandma Mary's two other children had moved there, and she had followed them. Dad's younger brother had accepted a job in Lancaster, Pennsylvania, and once or twice a year we visited him and his family.

My favorite holiday was Thanksgiving. Relatives came to our house for the holiday dinner. In the morning, my parents and Ruth drove to the Millburn High School football stadium to cheer for the Millers. They enjoyed the game but were most excited to watch me and the other twirlers perform at half time with the marching band.

TWO MONTHS AFTER RUTH DIED, I graduated from high school. On the last day of school, we received our yearbooks, and I scurried around to get as many teachers and classmates as I could to sign on their pictures.

After I got home, I went to my room and sprawled on my bed with the book. I opened it to the *Seniors* section and began reading the personal messages scrawled on many of the class pictures.

> *I admire you more than you realize.*
>
> *Love, kindness, and understanding are all characteristics you possess.*
>
> *Judy, you're a great girl from whom great things can be expected.*
>
> *All the luck in the world to a girl I've always liked and respected.*
>
> *You're a wonderful person who deserves life's best.*

I think you're great, what can I say?

So many nice words, so many platitudes. It was hard to take them all in.

Once I finished looking at the personal comments, I began leafing through the yearbook from the beginning, looking for other photos that included me. There was a photo of me with other class officers, another of me as one of three voted Most Versatile, and a spread on the majorettes.

Guess this is the book's sports section, I thought. I turned the page, gazed at the largest photo on the right page, and my heart stopped. It was of the crowd lining the white wooden fence and sitting in the bleachers at the last Thanksgiving football game. Fans were holding up cards that spelled out, *Millburn.*

Behind the fence, and in front of the seated crowd near the right edge of the picture, were the head and shoulders of a girl. She was slightly built, wearing a hat tied under her chin, with part of her dark, pixie-cut hair framing her face. She was looking up at the crowd, perhaps trying to spot her parents in the throng. They were probably watching their other daughter twirl her baton during the halftime show.

"It's Ruth," I whispered. I kept gazing at the photo. She was so beautiful, sweet, innocent. There she was, alive and reasonably well. At the time, we had no idea she would die five months later.

After

CHAPTER 7

THE FUNERAL, BURIAL, AND *SHIVA* PERIOD were a blur. Family and friends came and went. I felt numb. "How are your parents doing?" "How is your mother holding up?" "You're going to have to be strong for your folks."

When I think back, not one person asked me how *I* was doing.

I *did* have a spiritual experience that brought me some comfort. It was at the funeral home, an hour before the service began. An aunt and uncle had picked out the casket and made all arrangements, so the day of the funeral was the first time I'd been in the building.

A limousine transported Dad, Mom, and me the short distance from our house. It was a warm, sunny day in early May. I wore a black knit sheath with a matching jacket. Mom was also dressed in black, and Dad had on a dark suit with a white shirt and solid blue tie.

We didn't say anything during the seven-minute drive. I stared out the window as we approached the red brick building that resembled a large private home. It had a pair of black-shuttered windows on either side of the main entrance, and an awning covered the walkway from the front door to the sidewalk. A modern metal relief of a menorah hung above the set of windows on the right, and low shrubs graced the front.

We rode down a sloped driveway, and the driver stopped to let us out at the back entrance, on the lower level. Beyond it was a large parking area.

We passed the office and made our way up the stairs. The funeral director greeted us and took us into the family room to the right of the chapel. The dark green wall-to-wall carpeting and soft green patterned curtains on either side of the windows offered a feeling of comfort.

My mother gripped my father's arm, and he led her to one of the black-lacquered chairs, interspersed with couches and end tables, along the edge of the room. Mid-morning sunlight streamed in.

"I don't know how I'm going to get through this," Mom said. Dad looked pained and squeezed her hand.

My aunt and uncle walked in. They each leaned down to kiss my mother's cheek, then greeted my father and me. "How're you doing?" my uncle asked.

"Okay, I guess," Dad answered.

As they continued to talk, I left the family room for the chapel, entered, and closed the door behind me. The room appeared bigger than it actually was, thanks to several large windows on the outside wall; each was framed by soft beige drapes. The floor was covered with a honey-brown carpet, and there were two rows of wooden pews. In front and to the left, on a raised wooden platform, stood a simple wooden lectern; to the right, a round wooden table contained a large vase of yellow, burnt orange, and gold chrysanthemums.

In front of the platform, on a long, flat gurney, rested a simple wooden casket. I sat down on the nearest pew and looked at it. *I can't believe you're in there,* I thought. My eyes teared up, and I dabbed them with a tissue.

I was gazing at the casket when I witnessed an ethereal puff of purple smoke leave the box and rise upward. *It's Ruth's soul,* I thought. I felt certain at that moment that her essence had separated from her body. What was left in the casket was just a shell and some bones.

AFTER THAT, MY FIRST CLEAR MEMORY is visiting the grave with my parents soon after the week of *shiva* had ended. "We're going to the cemetery," my father said, "and we want you to come with us."

I didn't want to go but felt I had no choice.

It was another beautiful day. We climbed into the Chevy sedan, Dad and Mom in the front, me in the back. Our modest, three-bedroom Tudor sat on a hill, and the one-car detached garage was behind it to the left.

As Dad backed the car down the driveway and into the street, I noticed that the rock garden in front of the house was devoid of greenery and flowers. Mom usually plants in the spring. *It'll probably go by the wayside this year,* I told myself.

We drove a couple of blocks through the neighborhood, passing other Tudor and colonial-style houses and the southern end of Taylor Park. At the traffic light, we turned left onto Main Street and headed to the Garden State Parkway. Once on the highway, it took fifteen minutes to get to the cemetery.

When we left the Garden State, we passed a commercial area and residential one. After a couple of blocks, we entered the cemetery. There was no big sign, just a small marker.

Our newly-purchased family plot was in the section nearest the entrance. We turned right onto the first dirt road, right again, and parked midway down the gravel lane under a tree. It had gotten quite warm. Dad told me to open the back windows to prevent the car from getting too hot.

As I emerged, I felt a lump in my throat. I followed my parents to the new mound of earth under which Ruth's casket had been buried.

Our plot consists of six graves," Dad said. "Grandma Mary wants to be buried here, and maybe you and your future husband will use it. We ordered a simple headstone that'll be installed in a few months, along with a footstone for Ruth."

I nodded but couldn't say anything. The lump in my throat seemed bigger, and the rest of me felt numb.

My parents each picked up a small stone and told me to do the same. I followed their lead and placed my stone at the foot of the grave.

They stood before it, huddled together as one, and Mom was weeping. Dad motioned for me to come closer, but I couldn't. I stood stiffly apart. I felt like an outsider, physically unable to join them.

After they talked tearfully to Ruth for a few minutes, Dad took out a prayer book and together they recited the *kaddish*—the Jewish prayer for the dead.

While they did, I wandered up and down the nearby rows of graves, looking at the names and dates of Ruth's neighbors. When had they died? How old had they been?

Four members of one family had perished on the same day. The two children had been very young. A few days later, I went to the library, hoping to discover how they'd died but found no mention of them in the local newspapers.

DURING THE NEXT FEW WEEKS, we visited the cemetery several more times, and it was always the same. Mom and Dad stood close together. I buried my grief deep inside, unable to deal with it.

Ironically, many years later I found the cemetery a place of tremendous solace. When I was ready to recognize the intense pain of losing Ruth, I visited her grave a couple of times on my own. There was never anyone else around. With only a rustling of leaves and distant sounds of traffic in the background, I was able to tell her what I was feeling and begin to heal.

CHAPTER 8

R UTH HAD DIED THE END OF APRIL. After the mourning, I went back to high school and did my best to get into the rhythm of the final weeks of my senior year. Two girls in my class had lost their fathers around then, and every time I looked at one of them, I thought, *Her father just died.* I didn't realize that my classmates probably looked at me and thought, *She just lost her sister.*

Otherwise, everything at school was pretty much the same. There was the senior prom and graduation. I did simple clerical work in an office part of the summer and got together with the same group of friends. In August, we all got ready to go off to college in the fall.

At home, however, a new pattern emerged. Mom periodically got very weepy, and Dad consoled her. I read later that couples who lose a child either become extremely close or drift apart and eventually divorce. My parents formed a tight, almost impenetrable bond with each other.

Sometimes the three of us walked along Whittingham Terrace, the street that bordered Taylor Park—a lovely, thirteen-acre parcel of land a block from our house. Mom and Dad walked together, and I brought up the rear. I felt left out; although I could have said something, I didn't.

We passed the tennis courts and recreation building on the left and sometimes entered the park to circle the swimming (and ice skating) pond. In Spring, the cherry and dogwood trees bloomed, making it a favorite place for bridal parties to pose for photos.

Other things changed. One was my new feeling of vulnerability. Before Ruth died, I had loved to watch planes take off and land, and loved to fly. My dream, growing up, had been to be a pilot. I'd looked forward to our next flight with eager anticipation. We had flown to Florida a number of times, and I'd loved feeling the plane's tremendous thrust as it lifted off the ground. I had also enjoyed gazing out the window at the clouds. Even when there was turbulence, I had felt confident we'd reach our destination unharmed.

A few weeks after Ruth died, we flew to visit former neighbors who had moved to Michigan. It was a smaller plane than I was used to, with rows of two seats on either side of the aisle. My parents sat together; I sat across from them. There were storms along the route, and the plane hit many air pockets on its way. I was terrified. I clenched my fists and prayed to get there safely.

The flight home was uneventful, but anxiety consumed me. I repeated softly, over and over again, *Please let us get there safely.*

I flew many times after that, but my pre-flight and in-flight anxiety remained. On each trip, I prayed all along the way. When I reached my destination, I was always exhausted.

CHAPTER 9

NOT LONG AFTER MY SISTER DIED, my parents decided they could alleviate some of their grief by helping other needy children. The first summer after Ruth's death, they arranged through New York's Fresh Air Fund to have an inner-city child stay with us for two weeks. Her name was Sharon. She was twelve years old, had short blond hair, and was very sweet.

On the surface, I was welcoming, but underneath I felt furious. With Ruth gone, I wanted my parents all to myself. I didn't want to share them with anyone else. Sharon was also sleeping in my sister's old room and wearing some of her clothes. How dare she, and how dare *they?* I wondered. However, I kept all these feelings inside. *I must be a terrible person to feel this way,* I thought.

THAT SUMMER, MY PARENTS ESTABLISHED The Ruth Gottscho Kidney Foundation in memory of Ruth to help people in New Jersey with kidney disorders. They put together a board of directors composed of friends and professionals from within the community. Intellectually, I considered it a wonderful way to remember Ruth, and I applauded their efforts.

They and their friends organized fund-raisers and brought in several hundred thousand dollars. Over the next few years, the foundation improved the lives of countless kidney patients.

In the early 1960s, kidney dialysis became available for the first time. "If this'd been available a couple of years ago," my mom lamented, "it might have saved Ruth's life."

Initially, dialysis was only available on a limited basis at certain hospitals, and it was very expensive. Patients usually required treatment for three to four hours, three times a week. Medicare didn't cover it until 1973. Those patients who couldn't afford dialysis treatments to remove the toxins from their blood literally died.

One life-saving alternative was the use of home dialysis machines. They were lower in cost and less expensive to run, though they were still too prohibitive for many families on a limited income.

The foundation raised enough money to buy 180 home dialysis machines and lent them to kidney patients in New Jersey who couldn't afford to buy them. It also funded training for family members on how to use the machines. When a patient no longer needed the home dialysis machine—because he or she had received a transplant, or died—the machine was refurbished and lent to another needy patient.

Rocco, the genial principal of an elementary school, was the first person to receive one of these machines. Although he was unable to have a transplant, he enjoyed many productive years despite being dialyzed at home.

A pretty, soft-spoken homemaker named Micki, with a devoted

husband and two young adopted children, was another early recipient. She relied on home dialysis to keep her alive for several years until she received a transplant. "The foundation saved her life," said her grateful spouse. Altogether perhaps 250 people benefited from the home dialysis program.

On one level, I was in awe of how quickly the organization made such a difference in the lives of New Jersey kidney patients. But I was also very jealous of my parents' commitment to their "new baby." When asked, I gave lip service to what a wonderful thing they were doing. But I really wanted to shout at them, *After you spent so many years catering to Ruth and her needs, I now want your undivided attention.*

It didn't matter that I was away at college. I was still jealous of all the time they spent building that living memorial to Ruth. *It's selfish of me*, I thought. *I should be more supportive of what they're doing.* To the outside world I was. On the inside, I remained sad and angry.

Something else changed after Ruth's death. Although I had loved my sister with all my heart, I couldn't speak her name. For many years I referred to her only as "my sister."

CHAPTER 10

WHEN I WENT TO COLLEGE and met girls in my dorm, the question I dreaded most was, "Do you have any brothers or sisters?"

Initially I said, "No."

Some people knew me from home, though, so eventually I explained, as quickly as possible, "I had a sister, but she died."

Then after a while, I'd follow that stock reply with a quip: "So I know what it's like to be a sibling *and* an only child."

Some girls on my floor talked about their sisters with derision. One said she hated hers and didn't speak to her. It broke my heart. Although I didn't say anything, I wanted to yell, *You still* have *your sister, and I* don't. *I'd give anything to have mine back. How can you have a sister and not talk to her?*

As usual, though, I kept my feelings to myself.

In college, as in high school, I was a good student. I majored in English and minored in French. I became active in student government—ran for class secretary (and won), took ice skating lessons in the rink behind my dorm, rushed sororities (but decided against joining), and resumed piano lessons. At the end of my first year, I was invited to join the Cwens national honor society for outstanding freshman women.

It was a great distinction to be chosen, and those who submitted nominations were sworn to secrecy. It was a complete surprise when they knocked on my door early one morning, blindfolded me, stuck a gray hat with red lettering on my head, and led me in my pajamas to a breakfast for new inductees. I was speechless for a while, certain they had made a mistake.

Inside, I remained very melancholy. I'd brought a small phonograph to school and played my favorite records whenever I was blue. There was something about George Shearing compositions that were very soothing. I also listened to Rachmaninoff's "Piano Concerto No. 2" over and over again. Its plaintive passages, performed by Sviatoslav Richter, reached down to my core and provided a salve.

BOTH OF MOM'S SIBLINGS LIVED IN FLORIDA with their families, and we had visited them every year or two when Ruth and I were growing up. Mom and her brother, Sidney, were close, but she shared a special bond with her sister, Toby. At some point during each visit, Mom and Toby stood up and delivered a rousing rendition of the song, "Sisters, Sisters," written by Irving Berlin for the 1954 movie *White Christmas*. (In the movie, Rosemary Clooney and Vera-Ellen are the sisters, although Clooney sings both parts.)

In the song, the sisters declare their complete devotion to each other. Mom and Toby act out the words as they sing. The rest of the family greets the end of the performance with loud applause.

The first time Mom, Dad, and I visited the Florida clan after Ruth died, past history should have prepared me—but it didn't. One evening after dinner, all our relatives gathered in my aunt's living room. I was sitting on the floor with several cousins. As if on cue, Mom and Toby stood up and began singing their signature song.

The words hit me with a wallop and tore through my heart. I could hardly breathe. *If only I could push a button and drop through the floor*, I thought.

I glanced around and realized no one was looking at me or understanding how painful it was for me to listen.

My sister is dead, I wanted to scream. *Don't you realize that?* They were carrying on as if nothing had happened.

I THOUGHT IT WOULD GET EASIER, but two years after Ruth had died I was nowhere. Just after beginning my third year of college I wrote this poem:

> *Sometimes as I'm half asleep*
> *Your voice and laugh I hear so well*
> *And then we're talking very soft*
> *Just like before — and then the bell*
> *The clock goes off above my head*
> *It's two years now since you've been dead.*

So time had passed, but I hadn't begun to deal with losing Ruth. As in high school, when she was so sick, there was the exterior Judy and the interior Judy. Thus far, I had been able to keep them apart. Eventually, the wall between the two would come tumbling down.

CHAPTER 11

IN MY FIRST TWO YEARS OF COLLEGE, I had a total of five room-mates. In 1960, I was part of the largest freshman class to enter Penn State. The university had enrolled more new students than there was space for.

I spent the early months of my freshman year with three other girls in a student lounge that had been converted into a makeshift dorm room. It was painted hospital green, and a bed, bureau, and desk sat against each wall.

Audrey was gangly, with a thin, sharp nose and short, cropped hair. When the alarm rang each morning, she reached for the cigarette pack and lighter on the bureau just beyond her head and smoked a cigarette before getting out of bed.

Andrea was a plump, soft-spoken girl with dark hair and a serious expression. She couldn't countenance swearing or off-color jokes.

Loretta was my third roommate. She was very social, had short, curly brown hair, and was often down the hall chatting with friends.

The following January, Housing moved me around the corner into a regular dorm room. My new roommate was Leslie—a beautiful, smart senior with shoulder-length silver-blond hair. Most days, she was away from the dorm until bedtime.

In hindsight, living in a makeshift dorm room with three others who were very different from me and then with a senior absorbed in post-college plans afforded me the perfect opportunity to avoid forging close friendships with them. I didn't have to reveal the depth of my grief and loneliness.

In the beginning of my sophomore year, I moved to a more modern dorm with built-in wooden furniture. My roommate was Lindy, a short, friendly brunette with warm brown eyes and a ready laugh. This new relationship brightened my world, but I still never mentioned Ruth and the hole I felt inside.

Lindy transferred to the University of Pittsburgh in June. We remained friends, though I kept my grief and sadness under wraps.

IN MY JUNIOR YEAR, I FELT it was time to have a room of my own, though they were hard to come by. To increase the odds, another classmate and I persuaded Housing and the French department to let us designate a hallway in one of the centrally located dorms as "the French wing." Students who lived there had to converse only in French when they were on the hall or in their room. As the organizers, we each got to choose which room we wanted. I chose a single at the quiet end of the hall where I could study undisturbed in the early morning.

It was fun speaking French, but the language requirement provided another layer of distance. Once again, I formed only superficial relationships with those around me.

My social life left a lot to be desired during my first three years of college. In my senior year, I began dating Bill, a Canadian graduate student in electrical engineering. We'd met when a blind date, Al, suggested we join a friend and *his* blind date to hear a local band at a college nightspot. Bill was stocky and not much taller than I. He wore dark-rimmed glasses and spoke with a slight lisp, but he had an engaging personality. I liked him immediately, and all during the evening he and I communicated our mutual interest via eye contact and smiles.

He called me the next day and asked me out for the following weekend. We were amused to discover that Al had phoned the girl who had been Bill's blind date. We dated most of my senior year.

"My sister died three years ago," I told him early in our relationship. "I haven't told many people."

"I'm really sorry." He had a caring expression on his face, but I knew he didn't know what else to say.

I cried, and he held me. "I just wanted to tell you." We never talked about it again.

One thing I didn't do at Penn State was get counseling. Students could get psychological counseling for free. There was one counselor I'd heard was particularly good. I knew I needed to talk to someone but never drummed up the courage to make an appointment. After I graduated, I kicked myself many times for not getting the help I needed.

In my senior year, I had no idea what career I wanted to pursue. My dad arranged for the Klein Institute for Aptitude Testing to give me a series of tests.

The tests determined that I would be happiest in, and most suited for, a career in journalism, advertising, or music, and least suited for, or interested in, a business career. It also concluded that I was too self-critical, and that my ego needed boosting.

Even more important, the testing revealed something else:

"At the time of taking this test, Judith had the subject of health on her mind. . . . As a rule, whenever this appears in an individual's test responses, it is usually advisable to have a complete medical check-up to eliminate the possibility of any nervous, emotional, or organic involvements."

More than twenty-five years after Ruth died—when I began researching the effects of childhood sibling loss, I discovered it's very common for the surviving sibling to be unduly worried about his or her health. I took this battery of tests just three years after her death, but nobody connected the dots.

CHAPTER 12

IN THE BEGINNING OF MY SENIOR YEAR, I was accepted into Penn State's first study abroad program at Strasbourg University in France. I spent April through June in the lovely Alsace-Lorraine region of eastern France on the German border.

It should have been an exciting, carefree time—the culmination of my academic career. Instead, it was a period of acute anxiety accompanied by intense feelings of isolation.

I was extremely anxious on the plane. The flight from New York to Stuttgart was a nightmare. I didn't sleep a wink, since I was convinced I needed to stay alert for any emergency.

Instead, I wrote a "Dear John" letter to my boyfriend, Bill. In my letter, I gave all the reasons—real and manufactured—why I had to end our relationship. While almost everyone else on the plane slept, I filled sheets of thin white stationery with my ramblings:

Even though I care for you very much, I think
we need some space. With me in Europe and you

still at school, it's a good time to take a break.
Maybe we can reconnect after I get back. . . .

I was exhausted when the plane landed. After going through customs, we boarded a bus for the three-hour ride through the Black Forest to Strasbourg. We traveled on scenic mountain pathways through thick stands of pine that blocked the sun. I tried to enjoy the ride, but I worried that the bus was traveling too fast on the winding two-lane road.

Despite fatigue and lack of sleep, my first view of Strasbourg was magical. The university lay near the center of the city. We rode through narrow streets lined with residences and commercial buildings in varying shades of stucco and timber. Although French, there was a definite German influence—understandable since it's close to the German border and had been annexed by Germany during the war. Along the way, we also passed the imposing Gothic Notre Dame Cathedral, a dominating presence in the center of town.

We rode on to the university, one of the largest in France. The campus contained a variety of old and new buildings, one an imposingly long, low, gray stone edifice. Several were connected by paths that criss-crossed an expansive green quad.

It was late morning. The air was chilly, but the sun shone brightly. We got off and waited with our Penn State advisor for the driver to open the storage bin and unload our luggage. As he hefted the bags onto the ground, we grabbed ours and lifted or dragged them along to our dorm.

The first few days, I cried myself to sleep. In addition to being lonely, I was very constipated. It was a family problem that I'd had to deal with occasionally, but this time it seemed to last forever. I kept drinking apple juice, but nothing happened for well over a week. It never occurred to me to get a laxative at the local pharmacy.

Initially, I shared a large room with three other Penn State students. *Shades of my freshman year,* I thought. After several days, we moved to single rooms. Mine was very stark, and cockroaches were my constant companions. When I saw them scurrying around, I froze in fear. I gradually came to accept them as part of the living quarters—as did my fellow students. "Just part of the territory," one of them said.

The bed was similar to an army cot, with warm but drab-colored blankets. There was a simple table and chair, a free-standing clothes closet, and a window that opened onto a dingy courtyard.

I wrote to my parents every day—long, cheery letters on thin blue aerogram stationery. I couldn't believe they'd let me go to France, and I felt an obligation to keep them in the loop.

"If anything happens to you, I couldn't go on living," Mom had told me after Ruth died. The unwritten message had been to stay safe because Mom's life was in my hands. I know now that it was a tremendous burden to carry. At the time, I felt compelled to give them a detailed account of each day (with editorial license, of course).

I didn't know any of the girls in the program well, so I had no real buddies to hang out with. As usual, I got along with the other students but didn't bond with anyone.

EXCEPT FOR FRENCH LANGUAGE AND LITERATURE, our courses were taught in English and were just for those in the Penn State program. Because of this, we felt separate from the regular French students.

We'd stick together, going into town in groups of two or three and strolling down the narrow stone streets and along the canal. We usually stopped at a local *patisserie* for a *café au lait* and croissants or *tarte aux fruits*.

In addition to classes, there were organized day and weekend trips to local sites. One of the French teachers was a dashing, charming professor in his forties who invited two or three students at a time to take weekend excursions with him in his sports car. After the first couple of trips, word got around that he was a very fast, reckless driver. I was a scaredy-cat, so I vowed never to go with him. That summer, he was killed in a car accident. *Thank goodness no one had been in the car with him,* I thought.

One weekend I visited Baden-Baden with a classmate. The historic town lies just over the French border in southeast Germany—a half-hour train ride from Strasbourg. Pretty white stone houses with red roofs dotted the hills around it, on the edge of the Black Forest.

Baden means "baths," and there were more than twenty natural hot springs in the area. It had been named Baden-Baden to distinguish it from other towns whose names began with Baden.

We stayed at a lovely old bed-and-breakfast close to the middle of town. The streets were lined with stone buildings, boutiques, and open air restaurants. What I remember most about the B&B was the feather bed on which I slept. Goldilocks would have considered it "soft but not too soft, and deep but not too deep—just right." The bedding enveloped me, and I sank down into it and fell into a sweet, dreamless sleep.

But something I witnessed the following morning made me panic and want to get out of Germany as quickly as possible. Down the street from our B&B, a group of uniformed men lined up in formation. I immediately thought they were German soldiers, and that I, a Jew, was in danger. My mouth went dry, and I started to panic. I asked a local townsperson who they were and what was going on. "They're the fire brigade," he said in French with a marked Alsatian accent. "They're lining up to march in a local parade."

My relief was palpable, but I continued to feel an underlying unease about being in Germany.

No members of my immediate family had died in the Holocaust. My paternal Jewish ancestors had lived there but emigrated to the United States long before the lead-up to World War II. My maternal grandmother left Russia as a teenager shortly after the turn of the twentieth century to escape anti-Jewish pogroms.

I think my heightened vulnerability after Ruth died, as much as being Jewish, had exacerbated my fear.

That feeling of trepidation in Baden-Baden was nothing, though, to how I felt on a visit to Natzweiler-Struthof—the smallest of the German concentration camps and the only one currently on French soil. It sat on a hill in the Vosges Mountains, thirty-one miles southwest of Strasbourg, on what had been German-occupied territory during World War II.

One day, our Penn State faculty advisor had come into our classroom to announce the trip. "We've hired a mini-bus to take students to see a concentration camp that's been preserved as it was during the war," he'd said. "If you'd like to go, let me know." I had eagerly signed up. I'd felt it was important to see what one was like.

A dozen of us traveled to the camp a week later. It was a dreary, overcast day. Fear gripped me the minute we walked through the main gate. The high doors, wooden and wired, closed behind us, and I felt trapped. I was sure there'd be no escape. I started to sweat despite the cool weather. My heart began racing, and I struggled to keep my composure.

We went on a tour with other visitors—some with young children. While the youngsters ran around playfully, the guide led us past several stark wooden structures and told us matter-of-factly what they had been used for during the war. When she described the medical experiments that had been conducted in one building, I couldn't breathe. All I wanted was to get out of there. *How can the others seem so nonchalant?* I wondered in a panic.

After a while, I stopped listening to the guide and was relieved when the tour ended.

There was a gift shop where visitors could write a postcard and have it mailed from the camp with a Struthof postmark on it. I fingered some of the cards on display, and then paranoia and crazy thinking again set in. If I did this, I thought, I'll become a prisoner with no chance of escape. I breathed a sigh of relief when we boarded the bus and headed back to the university.

CHAPTER 13

A FTER CLASSES ENDED, I STAYED in Paris for several weeks in the summer of 1964. I lived at the Fondation des Ètats Unis—a low-cost residence for American students on the Cité Internationale Universitaire de Paris campus. The dormitory was an imposing six-story red brick building with cream-colored stone trim, one of forty separate housing facilities for French and foreign students. I had applied and been accepted a few months before I left for Strasbourg.

Soon after I got there, I ran into a couple of girls I knew from Millburn who were living in the same dorm. They'd come to Paris to study French for the summer.

Sometimes I hung out with them in one of our dorm rooms, ate with them in the cafeteria, and went with them to see some of Paris's many attractions. One of our first outings was to the Eiffel Tower. I was afraid of heights, so I stayed on the second floor when they took the elevator to the top.

All the French food was delicious, but I loved baked goods, *cafe au lait*, and the local yogurt the best. I was very thin all through school, so indulging in these treats was not a problem.

My favorite meal was breakfast. Even in the dorm cafeteria I could get a freshly baked croissant and a *cafe au lait*. I don't remember caffeine bothering me in Paris (it started to give me the jitters a few years later), perhaps because the French-pressed coffee was diluted with an equal amount of steamed whole milk. It was *très delicieux* sprinkled with cinnamon.

Along with the croissant I ate fruit-flavored yogurt. The French version was smooth and tasty. In America, the brand closest to it was Yoplait, but the yogurt produced in France was head and shoulders above that.

During the day, I often stopped at a *patisserie* for another *cafe au lait* and a slice of freshly baked fruit tart—as I'd done in Strasbourg. The thin buttery crust was topped with slices of fruit baked and then dusted with confectioners sugar. My favorite was rhubarb.

But the two Judys (exterior and interior) both remained very much present in Paris. I chose to be by myself a lot. Reading was my escape, and I stayed in my room and read for several hours each day. There was a library in the dorm. I gravitated toward historical fiction. I finished one volume and immediately began another. *Exodus* by Leon Uris was one I couldn't put down. Often I felt very lonely, though, and cried when no one else was around, consumed by a deep feeling of sadness.

Soon after I arrived in Paris, I saw a notice in an English newspaper that a newly-formed organization, Democrats Abroad for Johnson, was looking for a clerical assistant. A similar group had been organized in London. I knew there was an election coming up in the United States, and that Lyndon Johnson and Hubert Humphrey were running on the Democratic ticket.

They needed someone to answer phones, clip newspaper articles that mentioned the organization, stuff like that. There was no salary, but the person chosen would be reimbursed for transportation and lunch expenses.

I was a liberal Democrat and loved national politics. I called immediately to schedule an interview. The following day, I met a staff member and was accepted. The commute was easy via the Metro, and I only worked weekday mornings. The wood-paneled office had large casement windows in a lovely old building in the heart of the city. I sat at a big polished wooden desk that was bare except for the phone and the day's English and French papers.

Although someone always let me in, I was alone in the office much of the time. The phone rang occasionally. Most often callers asked for voting information. Few international votes were cast, because in 1964 U.S. citizens living overseas did not have the federal right to an absentee ballot. The organization also solicited donations for the Johnson-Humphrey ticket, and I responded to queries about where to send contributions.

While I was in Paris, friends of my parents suggested I contact their friends, the Liebermans. When I spoke to Mme. Lieberman on the phone, she invited me to their home the following Friday evening.

The Liebermans lived in one of several undistinguished low-rise gray stone buildings clustered together in a residential area of Paris I hadn't been to before. They lacked the character and charm I'd seen in other Parisian neighborhoods.

"Good *Shabbos*," Mr. Lieberman said when he opened the door.

I hadn't realized I would be joining them for their weekly *Shabbat* dinner. It was the one Jewish ritual they observed together as a family.

Monsieur and Madame Lieberman were an attractive couple in their forties with a daughter and son in their early teens. The apartment was much warmer physically than the exterior. The dining and living rooms each had an area rug and traditional furniture. Soon after I arrived, we sat down to dinner at a large, round wooden table.

After the Liebermans lit two tall tapers and recited the blessings for the *Shabbat* candles, wine, and *challah*, we were served a delicious, multi-course meal by a domestic helper. It included soup, fish, meat, salad, several cheeses, and an assortment of pastries.

Before sitting down at the table, we engaged in some preliminary conversation. But once we were seated, all four Liebermans turned their attention to the television on a metal stand in the corner. They watched the news and said hardly anything to me, or each other, during the meal.

AT THE END OF MY STAY IN PARIS, I asked for and received a letter of recommendation to give to the head of public relations at the Manhattan office of the Johnson-Humphrey campaign on the ground floor of the Statler Hilton Hotel. I worked there from the end of August until the election. Once again, I received no salary but was reimbursed for my transportation and lunches. I knew I'd have to get serious about job-hunting once the election was over.

In contrast to Paris, the New York political office was a constant hub of activity. There were two rows with five desks each and many chairs throughout the room. I answered phones and handled whatever clerical tasks needed doing. I loved the political atmosphere and looked forward to coming in each day.

A highlight was meeting Hubert Humphrey when he stopped by to say hello.

Our scintillating exchange was as follows:

"Hello, Senator, so nice to meet you."

"Thank you very much. I appreciate your hard work and support."

I asked someone to take a picture of me and the Vice Presidential candidate, and Mom and Dad hung it on the wall outside my bedroom.

Johnson won in a landslide. He would have been elected even if there had been no public relations office in Manhattan or Paris.

CHAPTER 14

FTER THE ELECTION, I MOVED into an apartment in mid-Manhattan with a high school friend and got a job as an editorial secretary on a trade magazine for school administrators. The content was pretty dry, but I amassed short writing and editing samples, which I kept in a portfolio.

Eighteen months later, I started looking for a more substantial writing job. One of the employment agencies I was registered with told me about an opening at AT&T Long Lines, the long distance and overseas branch of the telephone company. They were looking for a writer for the company's monthly employee magazine.

"The position's a reach for you," the placement counselor said, "but I suggest you apply anyway."

The AT&T Long Lines building was on Canal Street in lower Manhattan, near the Holland Tunnel. I met with the editor, Ralph Manna, who asked me to write a short article about the neighborhood as part of my application.

"Curtains in the Window" was the name of the piece I submitted. It was about the changing face of what had been an industrial area for many years. More and more people were moving into apartments and lofts on Lispenard Street and other nearby blocks.

Ralph liked it and scheduled an interview for me with his boss, Jim Brunson. "The job includes some travel," he said. "You'll be interviewing Long Lines employees in various parts of the country. Does that pose a problem?"

"No problem," I answered. My stomach had lurched at the thought, but outwardly I was cool and confident.

Ralph offered me the job, and I accepted. It came with more money and more responsibility. I figured I'd worry about my fear of flying when the time came.

I began writing for *Long Lines* magazine in October 1966. My first assignment was an article for the December issue on how Long Lines kept the long distance and overseas calls flowing seamlessly on Christmas—traditionally the busiest calling day of the year after Mother's Day.

I interviewed several employees involved in monitoring the grid. I learned what was involved technically, and what they had to do before and during the heavy calling period to keep calls flowing.

A light bulb went off in my head. Why not adapt the poem "The Night Before Christmas" to tell the story of how Long Lines maintains service on Christmas despite high calling volume?

I got excited about the project. I wrote the first stanza and showed it to Ralph. He thought it was a great idea and gave me the go ahead to continue.

ADELSON AND EICHINGER WAS THE GRAPHIC DESIGN firm hired to redesign *Long Lines* shortly before I became a staff writer, and Bob

Eichinger was the designer who worked with us. We met at my first staff meeting.

I noticed how well put together he looked in a subtle plaid suit, wide tie, crisp white shirt with a pointed collar (not button down), dark socks, and well-polished black shoes. He was not what one would call good looking, but I found him appealing. I also noticed he had great posture, an important attribute in my book.

He was tall and lean, with light brown hair, a wide mouth, and a nose that was slightly off center with a bump in the middle—probably the result of a sports injury. His eyes were green with flecks of gray, and almond shaped.

These observations were brief, and my mind didn't linger on them long. But I also took note of his firm handshake, direct eye contact, and warm smile when we were introduced.

At the time, I was in a long-distance relationship with a guy named Norman, an attorney who lived in Florida. We'd met on a blind date a relative arranged when I was in Miami visiting family. Norman and I had hit it off and visited each other several times that year.

Bob and I had an easy camaraderie and engaged in casual office banter. I particularly enjoyed his droll sense of humor.

A number of us in the public relations department worked in a large, open area in Room 911. I sat close to the door.

One day when he appeared, instead of walking to Ralph's office after saying hello, he sat down in the chair next to my desk. "The poem you wrote about the night before Christmas at Long Lines was very clever."

"Thanks" I said, feeling my face flush. "Somehow I thought of the idea, and it worked."

He lowered his voice. "Any chance we can get together for a drink one day after work?"

"Right now I'm seeing someone, so I don't think so. But thanks for asking."

"No problem." He got up from the chair and went to see Ralph.

I gazed at his back as he walked away. *I really like him,* I thought. *Would it be so terrible to go out for a drink?* I could have kicked myself.

Not long afterwards, Norman and I broke up and I was transferred to the AT&T Long Lines advertising department on another floor of the building. Bob's firm continued to design the magazine, but we no longer ran into each other at work.

I BEGAN TO HAVE ANXIETY OR PANIC ATTACKS shortly after I got my job at AT&T Long Lines. My heart started racing, I sweated profusely, and I wanted to flee from wherever I was at the time. It usually occurred when I felt trapped—in a meeting, a movie theater, or any other confined space.

Each attack came without warning, and all I wanted to do was run away from wherever I was and get home to what seemed like the only safe place. Every time, I fought the urge internally, and the struggle tired me. Eventually it passed, but it left me feeling like a wet dishrag.

The first time it happened was when the Long Lines editorial staff participated in an exercise to experience what it was like to be blind. There were about twenty of us. We filed into the department's small, dark multi-media studio, took a seat, and were each given a piece of dark fabric to use as a blindfold.

"Place the blindfold securely over your eyes, so you can't see anything," said the exercise facilitator.

I did as I was told and started to panic. Everything was black, and I felt a complete loss of control. I began to sweat. My heart started to race, and I thought I was going to die. I surreptitiously nudged the blindfold up slightly so I could see the light from the screen, but it didn't help. All I wanted to do was get out and run as far away as possible.

I managed to hold myself together until the program was over. As soon as we filed out, I headed for the ladies room, shut myself in a stall, and started crying silently. It took me several minutes to pull myself together. I finally calmed down, splashed cold water on my face, and returned to my desk.

These attacks seemed to come out of the blue. Once I was in the local library when I started to feel one coming on. At that moment, an acquaintance spotted me and came over to chat.

"Haven't seen you in a long time," she said. "What's happening?"

I felt sweaty, my heart began to pound, and I thought I was going to pass out. "Nothing much," I managed to reply in what I hoped was a normal tone of voice. "I really have to go, though, because I'm meeting someone and I'm late."

My goal in any panic attack was to get away from whomever I was with, or wherever I was, as quickly as possible.

When I went to the movies or a concert, I had to sit in an aisle seat close to the door. I needed to know I could escape to the ladies room or outside the building where I could concentrate on calming down. Getting through the attack was always hard work. I didn't confide in anyone about these episodes. Instead I suffered in silence.

Several months after the attacks began, I read about Claire Weekes' book *Hope and Help for Your Nerves*. The author was an Australian physician and scientist known for her work dealing with anxiety disorders. I went immediately to the local book store and bought a copy.

Beginning with the first sentence, I felt she was talking directly to me:

> *If you are reading this book because your nerves are "in a bad way," you are the very person for whom it has been written, and I shall therefore talk directly to you as if you were sitting beside me.*

I couldn't believe it. She knew me and what I was going through. I knew then and there that this book held the answer. I consumed the 180 pages in no time.

"The strength to recover is within you, once you are shown the way," she says early on.

Dr. Weekes explains how the nervous system works, and how fear generates panic attacks. When the symptoms occur, our natural reaction is to fight them as hard as we can, but that approach is unproductive. We also want to run away, are not accepting, and are impatient with time. Her remedy involves doing the opposite and is very simple: *You can cure yourself by facing, accepting, floating, and letting time pass.*

This made sense. I had been fighting the symptoms, and it wasn't working. I believed in her and was willing to try this new approach.

In the book, she makes sure the reader understands the four

steps she proposes and how to achieve them. It wasn't easy. Learning to float, not fight, took practice. But over a number of weeks the panic attacks were occurring less frequently. Eventually, I was myself again.

BUT I WAS STILL ANXIOUS MUCH OF THE TIME. When Ralph gave me my first writing assignment that involved air travel, I became so nervous I ended up getting sick and had to reschedule the trip.

For a feature called "Ages of Man" I had to interview four employees at different stages of life—teen, young adult, middle age, and retired. Each lived in a different part of the country, and I and a freelance photographer had to travel to their turf to meet with them. Somehow, I pulled myself together to complete the assignment.

I flew to a number of places in the country to do stories on other Long Lines employees: Hardy, Oklahoma, to do a piece on an equipment maintenance man and his wife, who ran a working farm; Lafayette, Louisiana, to cover a New Orleans plant supervisor and his wife at the yearly Cajun Crawfish Festival; and Mesquite, Texas, where the husband of a central office reports clerk competed in the rodeo.

Ralph said he was pleased with my work; so was I. But anxiety was never far behind. In addition, I suffered from excruciating pain during my monthly period. I managed to mask the anxiety most of the time and took Valium to relieve some of the severe menstrual discomfort. But I often called in sick.

After several months on the job, my boss gave me some discomfiting information. "You're doing a great job, but I was surprised to find out you've taken more sick days than anyone else in the public relations department."

    I vowed to myself to do better in the days ahead.

CHAPTER 15

ESPITE MY FREQUENT ABSENCES, I looked forward to the work week more than the weekend—-though it meant a forty-five-minute commute each way on a crowded crosstown bus and packed downtown Eighth Avenue subway. Work provided a comfortable routine, and I didn't have to reveal too much about myself.

On weekends, I usually got together with girl friends. We hung out at one of our apartments or went out to dinner or the movies, sometimes a singles mixer.

After living in New York City for a while, I joined a singles sports club. Members could sign up for day and weekend trips.

The first singles sports weekend I decided to try was a ski trip to Mt. Snow in southern Vermont. I bought a new ski outfit for the occasion. We could rent boots, skis, and poles there. I went without knowing anyone.

The chartered bus left from mid-Manhattan after work on a cold, winter Friday evening. I boarded, had my name checked off by the group leader, and took an aisle seat toward the front. Soon a nice-looking woman a few years older than I sat down in the seat across from me. We smiled at each other and exchanged small pleasantries.

As others boarded, she turned to talk to several of them. It was obvious they knew one another from previous trips. One of the passengers was a beautiful woman in her late twenties, with long gray hair. She had a radiant smile and seemed to know everybody. I couldn't believe she was completely gray at such a young age. My mother was very attractive with salt and pepper hair, but she was a generation older. This woman was so pretty and popular, I wished I could be her.

After everyone had boarded, the driver closed the door, shifted into gear, and we started rolling. Traveling through the Lincoln Tunnel, west on Route 3, and north on the Turnpike, I began to feel very lonely. My heart started to race, and my stomach felt queasy.

Twenty minutes later, we had left New Jersey and merged onto the New York Thruway heading north.

By then, my heart was racing even faster, and all I wanted to do was get off the bus. I broke into a cold sweat. The trip leader was sitting diagonally in front of me, and I leaned forward to get his attention.

"Look, I really don't feel well, and I want to get off," I told him. "I'll call my father to pick me up."

He looked at me in disbelief. "Really?" he asked.

I assured him I was serious. "I'll be fine. I just want to get off and go home."

He got up, spoke to the driver, and made his way back to me. "In ten minutes, we'll be coming to the Red Apple rest stop near

Tuxedo. We can let you off there."

"Good."

They decided to make it an unscheduled rest stop for everyone on the bus and announced the change. Ten minutes later, we pulled off the highway and parked near the entrance to the building. "We're stopping here very briefly to let a passenger off," the driver announced. "We'll be leaving promptly in ten minutes."

"You sure you'll be all right?" the trip leader asked.

"Yes," I said as I grabbed my small weekend suitcase from the overhead rack. "I just need to get some sleep, and I'll be fine."

Inside the rest stop I found a pay phone and dialed my parents' number. My father answered. "What's the matter?"

"I don't feel well, and I got off the bus. Can you pick me up at the Red Apple Rest?"

He paused a few seconds. "It'll take me forty-five minutes to get there. Use the pedestrian overpass and wait for me at the rest stop on the south side of the Thruway."

I hung up and looked out the window. In a short while, the others who had gotten off with me filed back on, the door closed, and the bus began to pull away.

I crossed over the highway, to the southbound rest stop and waited. I felt lost and lonely.

BY THE NEXT DAY, I WAS FEELING BETTER. I stayed at my parents' house for the rest of the weekend. Late Sunday afternoon, my father drove me the twenty minutes to the small bus terminal in Irvington, New Jersey, that badly needed renovation. Buses to Port Authority ran fairly often at that time of the weekend. He parked the car, and we waited outside at the end of the short queue.

I loved my father, but when we were alone together I sometimes felt awkward, so we didn't talk much. When we did, the conversation was usually devoid of anything meaningful. This time, we both remained silent.

As the minutes ticked by, something started welling up inside me. I tried to push it down and looked away. I kept thinking about the bus coming soon and taking me back to the city.

Suddenly I started to sob uncontrollably. "What's the matter?" he asked in alarm.

"I feel like I'm falling apart," I managed to say, swallowing gulps of air. A girl of about five, her mother, a preppy college student, and an older man in the line stared at me, but I didn't care. "I think I need help."

"Let's go back to the house and talk to Mom. She'll know how to find someone you can talk to."

As we returned to the car, I berated myself. *Why couldn't I handle this without my parents?* We didn't say anything as we drove back to Millburn.

When we pulled up next to the house, my mother rushed to the door. "What *happened?*"

"At the bus stop, I couldn't stop crying. I need to see a shrink. Daddy thought you might know someone."

"I'm so sorry," she said. "I wish we could help you, but at this point it'll be better if you talk to a therapist. I think Elise knows someone. I'll call her."

Mom got her friend on the phone, and she mostly listened to Elise talking at the other end. "Uh-huh . . .yes, okay, give me her number. . . . Can I call her now?"

When Mom got off the phone, she said Elise had given her the name and number of someone she really liked. She dialed it.

When the woman answered, Mom explained it was an emergency and wondered if she could see me that night. The therapist asked her where I lived. When Mom said, "Manhattan," the therapist said it would be better for me to see someone in the city. She highly recommended Nohmie Myers, a colleague who had an office on East Eighty-sixth. Through the phone I could hear her give Mom Nohmie's phone number and say, "Have your daughter call her to make an appointment."

Mom handed me the phone and number, and I dialed it. A woman with a warm, mellow voice answered.

I apologized for calling on Sunday. I told her who had recommended her and explained that I couldn't stop crying and needed help. "Is there any chance you can see me tomorrow?" I asked. "I work, but I can call in sick."

"I can see you tomorrow afternoon at two."

"That's great."

"We'll pay for the therapy sessions," Mom told me.

"Thanks."

I decided to stay over one more night and return to my apartment in the morning. I felt like a little girl as I ate cookies and drank milk while watching television with my parents in their bedroom. We didn't talk much. I looked forward to my first therapy session with some trepidation but also eagerness. The next step in my life was way overdue.

CHAPTER 16

I SAT BACK ON A COMFORTABLE brown velvet-covered chair opposite Nohmie Myers, and we gazed at each other without speaking. Her office was warm and inviting. Soft greens, rusts, tans, and browns dominated. Paintings in muted colors graced the walls. It was spacious yet cozy. *I think I'm going to like it here*, I thought.

It was my first therapy experience. As we sat there, I felt expectant, not intimidated. I came in time to realize that therapy sessions often began that way. She was waiting for me to say something. I felt tongue-tied as I struggled to find the right words to describe my recent sadness that sometimes led to despair.

She was in her early forties, of average height, with short black hair that framed her round face and brown eyes that maintained their focus through black-framed glasses. She looked trim in a soft gray suit and comfortable black shoes. She maintained good posture, leaning forward in her chair and resting her hands in her lap.

Finally, she broke the ice. "So, Judy, tell me what brought you here." She had a mellifluous voice.

I knew I had to dive right in and not waste time. "I'm getting these panic attacks and crying jags, and I don't know why. I'm also anxious about a lot of things and can't seem to relax. Really, a lot of the time I'm fine, and then something happens. . . ."

"When you called last night, you said you had been crying uncontrollably. Can you tell me what happened just before that?" She looked directly at me with undivided attention.

"Well, I was at my parents' and had slept a lot. I was supposed to be in Vermont on a singles ski trip, but I started feeling sick right after the bus left Port Authority after work on Friday. I called my father to pick me up at a rest stop, and he drove me to my parents' house in Millburn. On Sunday, I was feeling okay, but when I was waiting with my father to take the bus back to the city I suddenly burst into tears."

"Do you remember what you were feeling just before you began crying?"

"Lonely. I wanted to go back to my apartment and go to work today—I really like my job—but I was feeling so cut off from my parents. . . . At least I think that's what I was feeling. I don't know, lonely, guilty. . . not really sure."

"You mentioned your dad picked you up at the rest stop and took you to the bus. What about your mother?"

"Oh, she's definitely there, too. It just so happened he picked me up, and he's the one who usually takes me to the bus."

"Tell me about your family. Do you have any brothers or sisters?"

There it was. I could feel my face flush. "My sister died when she was fifteen and I was seventeen. She was sick her whole life with kidney disease. That was seven years ago. I've only had these attacks more recently."

"That experience can be very hard on families," Nohmie said. "Everyone in the immediate family feels the loss very deeply, and it's often very hard to talk about."

I felt her empathy and was grateful.

We talked more about my family and my work, and soon it was the end of the session. The time had flown by.

"For the first month or so I'd like to see you twice a week," Nohmie said. "Then we'll cut back to once."

"Do you think I'll be okay?" I asked. "Will I get better?"

"Absolutely. But for now, I want you to call me if you start crying again like you did yesterday, or you have some other kind of emotional crisis."

"Thanks, I will."

She jotted down in her appointment book the next few dates she was scheduling for me, wrote them on an appointment card, and handed it to me. I collected my handbag and jacket, and left. I was feeling much better.

Shortly after I got home, the phone rang. It was my mother. "How'd it go?" she asked.

"Okay. I like her."

"Can you tell me what you talked about?"

"Oh, it's hard to remember. . . . How I was feeling, mostly."

"When will you see her again?"

"On Thursday, and then two times a week for the next month."

At that point, it seemed as if my mother had run out of questions to ask, and I didn't want to get into it further. We talked a little more about other things, but I became impatient and wanted to end the conversation. Soon, we said goodbye.

After I hung up, I felt guilty. They're paying for my therapy, I told myself, so I should be more forthcoming. But I wanted to keep what I said private.

A light bulb went off in my head: *If I want to keep what I say in therapy private, I need to pay for the sessions myself.* I'd have to talk to Nohmie about that. I had no idea how much it cost. I hoped I could afford it.

The next time we met, I told her I felt uncomfortable about my parents paying for my therapy. "I don't want to tell my mother what we talk about," I said, "so I think it's better for me to pay for my sessions."

"That's a good decision, and I can work with you on making my services affordable." She offered me a reduced rate that was manageable, and I was grateful.

OVER THE NEXT FEW WEEKS, she and I talked about my relationship with my parents. There was a lot of give-and- take. It wasn't psychoanalysis, where you lie on a couch and do most of the talking—often using free association—and the psychoanalyst listens and takes notes.

We would talk about a specific incident, and she would help me understand why I behaved a certain way. It became clear that I was scared of getting my parents angry—particularly my mother. I didn't have to be with them either to feel their anger—they were constantly in my head.

I didn't have much confidence or self-esteem, despite being successful at work and having friends. I was extremely hard on myself.

I felt that, if I made one misstep at work, I would lose my job, and if I said one wrong thing to my mother or father, they would disown me.

As THE WEEKS WENT BY, I started to feel stronger psychologically and assert myself more—especially with my parents.

When Dad took a business trip, Mom usually travelled with him. She didn't like to stay home alone. One day, he called to say he was in the city and would like to come over to ask me something. I said sure; he arrived a short time later.

I opened the door, we gave each other a kiss, and he came in and sat down. "How's it going?" he asked. "How was your trip to Philadelphia?"

I had spent the previous day at the Philadelphia Zoo with a Long Lines manager, his wife, and their three-year-old daughter. A freelance photographer had accompanied us. It was a beautiful day, and the little girl had had a ball looking at all the animals. The photographer had gotten some terrific shots of her feeding them, clapping when looking at the seals, waving at the penguins, and displaying some trepidation in the presence of a couple of large caged animals.

"It went well. I'm writing the story, and it's very challenging to try to make it interesting. I think it'll turn out to be less copy and more photos. . . . What did you want to ask me?"

"I need to go to Chicago next weekend to attend a planning meeting for the upcoming packaging show. Mom doesn't feel like going, so I'm hoping you'll stay with her while I'm gone. You know she doesn't like staying alone."

I swallowed hard, and my heart started racing. "I can't do it,"

I said.

" . . . Why not? You have plans you can't change?"

"No, I just think Mom has to learn to stay by herself for a couple of days. I can't always be her babysitter. I don't want to do it any more."

My face flushed, and I could feel my hands getting sweaty. My heart was pounding. I gazed at the floor, feeling like a terrible person.

". . . Well, I'm very disappointed in you," he said. "I ask you to do a simple thing, and you say you can't do it. . . . Let me rephrase that—you *won't* do it."

I felt awful. I didn't want him to be angry at me, but I said nothing.

"Okay, that's it, I guess." He got up, grabbed his coat from the chair, and marched to the door. I said goodbye, and he left without a kiss.

My mother never said a word to me about it. A couple of days later, she told me she was going to Chicago with Dad.

"I felt so guilty after he left," I told Nohmie the next time I met with her. "If my mother had been sick or something, that would have been different."

"No need to rationalize," she said, and I knew I had done the right thing.

A FEW MONTHS LATER, I AND A COLLEGE FRIEND, Judy, who also lived in Manhattan, planned a weekend trip to Washington, D.C., to visit another college friend, Sherri, a graduate student there. I told my parents *only* that I was going away with a friend for the weekend, not *where*.

"I'll call you periodically, so you know I'm all right," I reassured them.

"Can't you at least tell us what *city* you're going to?" my mom asked in a sweet, demure voice.

"We're taking the train and will be back Sunday night."

We boarded at Penn Station, and Sherri met us at Union Station and drove us across town to her apartment. While we chatted in the car, all I could think of was calling my parents to reassure them that I was okay. I did it soon after we arrived.

"Can I use your phone?" I asked Sherri.

"Sure, it's in the bedroom."

I closed the door and called home. "Hi, Mom, I just want you to know I arrived, and all is okay."

"You still don't want to tell us where you are?" she asked.

"No. I'll call you sometime tomorrow."

I did the next day, at least twice, and one more time before we got on the train for the return trip.

In therapy, I told Nohmie with a bit of embarrassment about my clumsy foray into independence. She and I laughed about it, because I had already realized I'd set it up so that precisely the opposite actually happened. By calling them all the time, I was holding on to the apron strings. To the extent I had, I'd spoiled having a good time with my friends.

CHAPTER 17

A FTER WRITING FOR *LONG LINES* FOR A YEAR, I was transferred to the company's advertising department on the eleventh floor. Dan "Hutch" Hutchins, the advertising director, had asked that I join his staff. AT&T Long Lines was sponsoring a TV special on NBC featuring comedian Bill Dana as the Hispanic-American character Jose Jimenez. In the show, *Discover America with Jose Jimenez,* the character travels throughout the country visiting American festivals.

My assignment was to write a story for *Long Lines* featuring him at the McKenzie River Salmon Festival in Eugene, Oregon. It was held annually in early April to kick off the salmon-fishing season.

I was one of five staff members who had desks in a small windowless area outside Hutch's private office. For the most part, the advertising department was very low key. Hutch didn't micro-manage. If you did your job, it didn't matter when you took your lunch or how much you chatted on the phone.

But in some ways it was too relaxed. Our young, pretty administrative assistant spent most of her time planning her wedding. The sales manager, who sat behind me, often chatted with his friends over the phone. Sometimes he'd put his feet on the desk and lean his chair back against the wall. The assistant advertising sales manager often clipped his nails.

I traveled to Oregon for the Salmon Festival with a couple of the guys from the advertising agency. We had separate cabins. We took two flights to get to Eugene, which made me anxious. I also wasn't super comfortable traveling with men I didn't know well.

Despite my trepidation, the trip to Oregon was wonderful. The McKenzie River, and the forest through which it flowed, were breathtaking. Douglas fir—the Oregon state tree—was dominant, along with several other species of fir, cedar, pine, and hemlock. I can still recall their intoxicating aroma. The cabins were constructed completely of lumber from local trees and had decks that jutted out over the water. The rustic buildings were cozy inside. Each had a stone fireplace, and someone from the cabin staff entered quietly early each morning to light the fire so the room was warm when you got up. The first night, I was uncomfortable keeping my door unlocked. But the rushing water was constant and soothing, allaying my fears.

The film crew remained on location for several days, shooting the preparation leading up to the festival, the many people involved in putting it together, and the flotilla of boats that traveled down the river to formally open the fishing season. I didn't have much personal contact with Bill Dana; I interviewed him for the story, but he and his retinue remained apart from the rest of us most of the time. My article appeared in the May issue, just before the show aired.

I can still remember the sound of the rushing water, the smell of the forest, and the beauty of the surroundings. *This is as close to Paradise as I'm ever going to get,* I thought. I vowed that some day I'd return to share the place with my husband, whoever he might be.

SHORTLY AFTER I RETURNED FROM OREGON, Mom called to tell me that my father needed surgery. He was a robust man of fifty-two when he developed a blockage in his colon. Although his hair was thinning, he only wore glasses for reading and walked with a rapid gait. Despite his occasionally brusque manner, I adored him.

I'd also become very angry at him at times when I was growing up. If I got into an argument with my mother, he sided with her, even if I was right.

Once, after losing an argument, I stomped out of the house and slammed the front door. "I'm *outta* here!" I screamed.

I immediately felt remorse and knocked repeatedly to get back in. "I'm coming, I'm coming," he said as he rushed from the kitchen. Then I heard a loud thud as he slipped on the tiled floor in the foyer and landed on his back. He struggled to open the door, in obvious pain. I was mortified and felt tremendous guilt.

Dad was a very successful packaging engineer who developed the first inline marking and coding machines. They revolutionized product packaging by enabling bottles and boxes to be marked with a code or other information as they moved automatically down the packaging line and into cartons.

When the government began *requiring* that all packaged foods be dated and contain other information, his business really took off. In recognition of his leadership in the industry, he was voted into the Packaging Hall of Fame.

Dad loved to sail, and one of my favorite memories was when he and I drove to the Jersey shore to rent a sailboat for the day. We rode down the Garden State Parkway with the top down on the only convertible we ever owned, the wind whipping through my hair.

I had learned how to sail at Camp Eagle Island. "Take the tiller and bring her about," he said several times. I'd exchange places with him and keep us on course for a while until he took over again. At the end of the afternoon, he let me sail back to the dock.

The surgery was performed in New York, and the pathology report came back the following week. Mom was very upset when she called me. "The news isn't good," she said. "Your father has cancer, and it's spread. But we're not going to tell him or anyone else. As far as he's concerned, it was a benign growth and they took it all out."

I couldn't believe she wasn't going to tell him the truth. " . . . Mom, are you sure that's the right thing to do?"

"If he knows the truth, he'll start feeling and acting sick. If other people know, they'll have him on his death bed."

I was too worn out to argue with her. I gave my word I wouldn't tell anyone. Almost immediately, I developed a bad cold. I was coughing and blowing my nose. I felt miserable.

When friends asked about the test results, I said, "The lab report was negative."

"That's great. Now you can rest easy."

"Yeah."

Maintaining secrecy was draining. I tried to get involved with my work, but it was difficult.

Five days later, my mother called, intent on relieving the burden.

"I want you to know I just told him the truth—that the tumor was malignant, but they got it all out."

As soon as she told me, my cold symptoms disappeared, but I was still upset. "That's *not* the truth," I countered. "You didn't tell him the cancer had spread."

She never *did* tell him, and I kept quiet. I wanted so much to talk frankly to my father about his prognosis, so he could be a major player in determining the best course of action.

Several months after the surgery, my parents traveled to Duke University to consult with Dr. Walter Kempner. He was famous for developing a rice diet that reduced obesity and promoted a healthy lifestyle, and he was confident he could build up Dad's immune system. After several weeks there, Dad *did* feel better. He lost some weight and had more energy.

Coincidentally, New Jersey Governor Richard Hughes was there with his wife, Betty. She was obese and lost many pounds under Dr. Kempner's care. My parents and the Hugheses became friends, and my father worked with the governor to pass legislation that provided improved state health care coverage for people with kidney disease.

Once, before he got sick, I asked him what I should do with the foundation if anything happened to him and Mom. We were taking a walk together. "I'm not sure I'd be able to keep it going without you," I confessed.

"Even if the foundation doesn't continue," he said, "it will have helped a great many people with kidney disease."

I felt a burden lift from my shoulders. The question had been on my mind, and I felt good that I had finally asked it.

CHAPTER 18

IN OCTOBER 1968, I RETURNED TO MY former desk in room 911—-this time as a writer for the company's *Management Report*. Emory Wilbur, the editor, had been handling the monthly publication by himself and needed help.

When I was a *Long Lines* staff writer, I'd had little contact with Emory—though his desk was just to the left of mine. He was a man of few words and fewer smiles. He worked quietly while others in the room chatted or congregated from time to time to shoot the breeze.

I wasn't thrilled with the new assignment. Matters dealing with management seemed dry and uninteresting. But I was happy to rejoin some of my former colleagues still working in that office.

When I returned to 911, I also saw Bob Eichinger again. His graphic design firm was still designing *Long Lines,* and he still came in to consult with Ralph. Bob looked just as dapper in tailored suits, crisp solid shirts, and tasteful ties. The first time he saw me sitting at my former desk, he greeted me with a warm hello and wide grin.

"Glad to see you're back," he said.

"Thanks." I smiled, and my heart did a flip.

Several days later, there was a goodbye party after work for Jim Brunson, the Long Lines Vice President for Public Relations, who was being transferred to another part of the country.

The event was held at Longchamps at Forty-second and Lexington, part of a chain known for its cocktail bar and light French cuisine. The owner of the original restaurant, at Seventy-eighth and Madison, was a race horse enthusiast who'd named it after the Paris track.

I made my way through the front door and down a curved staircase to where the party was being held. Red, black, and gold predominated, along with mirrors that made the underground space seem bigger. Red tablecloths covered the buffet tables along the walls. They were laden with platters of cheese and crackers, crudités, shrimp and cocktail sauce, and a number of hot appetizers. Soft drinks sat on a separate table, and a cash bar stood in one corner.

A few tables and chairs were scattered around, but most people were standing in small groups, balancing a drink and plate of snacks while they chatted.

I surveyed the crowd. A number of my colleagues were already there, along with many from upper management. I noticed Bob, across the room, talking to a couple of magazine writers. My heart again skipped a beat. I said hello to several people I knew standing nearby, poured a glass of club soda, and added a twist of lime. I wasn't ready to eat anything. It was too hard to juggle the plate, glass, and napkin.

For a while, I made small talk with a couple of newspaper people while I sipped my drink. Then I walked over to survey the food. I was trying to decide what to eat when Bob came over. "The shrimp are pretty good," he said. "The sauce isn't too spicy. I also recommend the stuffed mushrooms."

"Okay, I'll try them." I helped myself to a couple of each.

"They *are* good," I said after tasting them.

"You happy to be back in 911?" he asked.

"Not crazy to be writing for *Management Report* but happy to be back at my old desk," I said inanely.

"I liked the story on the salmon fishing festival in Oregon," he said. "What's Bill Dana like?"

"A funny guy, less of a prima donna than some other TV stars."

We chatted for a few more minutes, and then some others came over. Soon we were each talking to different people and drifted apart.

I ate more appetizers, had another soft drink, and chatted with a number of folks. One of them was the honoree, Jim Brunson. He was tall and lean, with a full head of salt- and-pepper hair—a handsome middle-aged guy who spoke slowly with a Southern drawl, as if he had all the time in the world. He remembered interviewing me for my job on *Long Lines* and said some nice things about my work. I wished him luck in his new position.

The whole time, I was aware that Bob was still there, across the room. Finally, people began to leave. I had decided I would time my departure with his, if I could.

I made sure to work my way over to where he was.

"Guess the party's winding down," he said.

"Yeah, looks like it."

"Where do you live?" he asked

"Thirty-seventh, between Third and Lex."

"I'm on East Forty-eighth. I'm gonna get a cab, and I can drop you off along the way."

"That'd be great." My heart was pounding.

We walked up the stairs and out to the street. He flagged a cab, and we got in. He gave the driver my address. I lived only five blocks away, and we reached the front of my building in no time. Bob was sitting on the sidewalk side, so he opened the door, got out, then turned to take my hand as I emerged onto the pavement.

"Thanks for the ride," I said. I waved goodbye and let myself into the building. Bob got back in the cab, and it drove away.

Soon, I was berating myself. *Why didn't I invite him in?*

Later, when we started dating and compared notes, he told me he had chided himself, also, for an opportunity missed.

Why didn't I invite her to dinner? he'd asked himself.

HE CALLED THE FOLLOWING EVENING. "Hi, how're you doing?"

"Fine. What about you?"

"Okay. We're finishing up the December issue of *Long Lines,* and it looks pretty good, but there's nothing in it that compares to the 'Night Before Christmas at Long Lines' poem you wrote two years ago."

"I still can't believe I pulled that off. Somehow, I got into a groove, and it worked."

We chatted a bit more, and then he said, "Hey, would you like to go out to dinner on Friday?"

"Sure, that would be great."

"I thought we'd go to the Grenadier at Forty-ninth and First. My partner's been there, and he said the food's good and it has a nice atmosphere."

"That's fine."

"Okay if I pick you up at seven?"

"Perfect. My apartment's 2A. We don't have a doorman, so I'll buzz you in."

"See you Friday," he said, and we hung up.

I felt light-headed and slightly giddy. There was something about him that I really liked. I was excited and nervous at the same time.

AS IT TURNED OUT, I WAS UNDER a lot of pressure at work Friday morning. Writing for *Management Report* was challenging, and the article I was doing had to be in by the end of the day.

Before going out for a quick lunch, I stopped in the ladies room. While washing my hands, I looked in the mirror. My lips were devoid of color, and my skin looked sallow. I'd better freshen my makeup after lunch, I thought.

I waited for the elevator. When the doors opened, Bob got out. He was carrying a large package under his arm.

"Hi," he said as he held the door for me. "I'm delivering the final mechanicals to Ralph."

"I'm running out to get a sandwich." I stepped into the elevator. "See you later."

"See you." The doors closed.

I look awful, I thought. I bet he took one look at me and regretted asking me out.

WHAT SHOULD I WEAR? I asked myself when I got home. I tried on several outfits and settled on a gray sleeveless wool dress with flecks of orange, that had a matching coat.

Before dressing, I carefully did my makeup. I looked in the mirror when I was done. A whole lot better than earlier today, I concluded.

Bob arrived promptly at seven. "You look nice," he said when I opened the door. I was wearing just the dress at that point.

"Thanks." I invited him in while I went to gather my coat and pocketbook.

"This is a nice apartment," he said, looking around.

It was an L-shaped studio, and I liked it a lot. I most loved the view from the window. I faced the courtyard, in which stood a large tree. A view of those branches greeted me every morning when I opened the blinds. I loved seeing the green leaves turn yellow in autumn and fall to the ground just before winter arrived. Even when the branches were bare they were beautiful, especially when tinged with a thin layer of snow.

"What's it like out?" I asked Bob as we were leaving the apartment.

"A little nippy." He helped me put on my coat, and I locked the door.

CHAPTER 19

WE TOOK A CAB TO THE RESTAURANT. Traffic was light, and we covered the fifteen blocks in less than ten minutes. My window was open a sliver, the cool breeze ruffling my hair.

The driver let us off at the front door. Inside the Grenadier, red predominated. Just past the bar against one wall sat tables for two with banquette seating on the inside and sleek black wooden chairs facing them. The maitre d' led us to one of these tables and pulled it out for me to slide in. He moved it back into place, then pulled out Bob's chair for him. When we were comfortably seated, he handed us menus and said, *"Bon appétit!"*

Our waiter appeared and we ordered white wine for me and a martini, on the rocks with a twist, for Bob. He took out a pack of cigarettes, offered me one—I declined—and lit one himself.

"How'd you like Jim's party?" he asked.

"It was pretty nice. Jim's a great guy. Even though I don't see him often, I'm gonna miss him. I love that Southern drawl and easy manner. Where'd he grow up?"

"Georgia, I think."

". . . How do you like designing the magazine?"

"Very much. Ralph's easy to work with. He doesn't micro-manage. It's fun to put together."

"By the way, whose idea was it to put a picture of me in the back of the issue with my zoo story?"

My photo essay had appeared in the previous August issue. The photographer had taken a picture of me pushing the stroller while the Long Lines employee featured in the piece chased after his daughter, who was running toward the duck pond. The photo had appeared in the monthly column, "Sidelines," in the back of the publication. It includes short vignettes related to the main stories. In the caption, I was identified as a "miss still enjoying single bliss."

"It was my idea," Bob confessed, blushing. I noticed how green his eyes were beneath hooded eyelids. They went well with the straight, medium brown hair.

The waiter served our drinks, and Bob stubbed out his cigarette. I didn't mind him smoking, though I wasn't crazy about the smell.

He had known he wanted to be an artist when he was six. "I hoped to be a cartoonist or an illustrator," he said, fingering his glass. "I graduated from the Rhode Island School of Design and was drafted into the army. After basic training, they assigned me to the army's graphic arts department on Governor's Island. That's where I met my partner, Dick Adelson. We designed all kinds of graphic materials and had a great view of the tip of Manhattan Island from our studio."

"I majored in English and French at Penn State," I said. "I had no idea what I wanted to do. I thought maybe public relations. My first job was at Buttenheim, on Third and Forty-seventh. I was an editorial secretary for a magazine about office and school furniture, of all things."

Bob chuckled.

"Wasn't very glamorous, but I came away with some writing samples, and Ralph hired me as a copywriter for *Long Lines*. I still can't believe it."

"You're a good writer," Bob said.

"Not really. Ralph does a great editing job."

When a waitress came to take our order, we hadn't even looked at the menu. We took a few minutes to choose—salads as an appetizer, duck *a l'orange* for me, and a steak for him.

After she left to place the order, I looked to my left and saw the maitre d' leading two young women to a table. As they passed us, one of them said hello. It was Rita, a woman who worked in room 911 as a writer on the newspaper.

"Well, if we want to keep our personal life separate from work, we may not be able to," Bob commented.

Soon, the salads came. As we ate, we talked about where we'd grown up—Bob in Bridgeport, Connecticut, and I in Brooklyn until I was eight, then Millburn. I told him how my sister had been sick her whole life and died at fifteen when I was seventeen. He said he was sorry to hear it.

He'd also had a tremendous loss growing up. "When I was thirteen, my mother died suddenly of what we think now was a brain aneurysm. At the time we thought it was a stroke. She began screaming in pain and went to bed. She died the next day. My father and Aunt Dolly, Mom's sister, felt it was better for me to stay out of the way. I was frightened. Nobody told me what was going on."

"That's kind of what happened to me. When my sister was dying in the hospital, my parents sent me to the cafeteria with one of their friends. When we came back, she was gone."

Bob's father married a single woman, his neighbor, a year later. It was her first marriage, and she loved Bob as if he were her son.

We talked and talked. Conversation was easy. We were sipping coffee—decaf for me and regular for him, when Rita came by again as she was leaving, looking straight ahead.

I glanced at my watch and was shocked to discover we'd been talking for two and a half hours. We could have continued the conversation for hours more without running out of things to say.

We left the restaurant shortly after ten. It was cooler but still pleasant, so we walked the fifteen blocks back to my place. He held my hand, and I liked it.

"I had a great time tonight," he said as we approached my building.

"I did, too."

"You like to do it again sometime?"

"Sure."

"How 'bout next Saturday night?"

"Sounds good."

"We could have dinner in the Village and walk around."

I was feeling lightheaded—as if I was floating.

We paused in front of my building. "Thanks again. I had a *wonderful* time," I said.

"I'll call you during the week." He bent down and kissed my

lips lightly, said goodbye, and I went upstairs. Once again I hadn't invited him in. *What am I, a moron?*

BOB CALLED TWICE DURING THE WEEK, and we spoke at length each time. At some point he asked, "Did Rita say anything about seeing us at the restaurant?"

"Not a word," I said. "She acted as if it never happened."

"Just curious."

He told me he loved to cook and prepared a complete meal for himself every evening he was home. "It usually includes meat or chicken, potato or rice, a veggie, and salad." There was no vegetable that Bob didn't like.

"Once or twice a week, I meet my buddies, Dick and Mort, for drinks after work," he continued. "After one or two martinis, we usually order something to eat, often a hamburger."

"My cooking repertoire is much more limited," I confessed. "It revolves around chicken. I keep chicken parts in the freezer and take out one or two pieces in the morning to defrost. I do a green vegetable or rice, and a simple salad to go with it. I'll make you dinner sometime," I blurted out and felt my face get hot.

"I'd like that."

NOT ONLY HAD MY SOCIAL LIFE taken a turn for the better, things were improving at work as well. Emory—whom I'd always described as stone-faced, cold, and distant—turned out to be a terrific mentor. He exercised infinite patience when explaining something to me, especially why he had made changes in the pieces I submitted for *Management Report*. I was not familiar with business terminology, and he was eager to teach me the lingo.

He also had a very nice smile, which he displayed often when we talked. He told me he was married and had a teenage daughter. I never would have pegged him as a family man. *Live and learn*, I told myself.

IT WAS WARMER ON SATURDAY, an Indian summer day, despite nearing the end of October. For my date with Bob, I decided to wear one of my favorite dresses—a simple deep purple A-line with short sleeves. I wore it often and always felt good in it.

Bob remarked on it when he arrived, "I remember you wearing that dress to work. It's a great color."

"Thanks. You look very spiffy." He was wearing a black-and-white plaid blazer, dark gray trousers, light blue shirt, and a colorful tie.

"Before we leave, do you mind if I take a look in your freezer?"

"Of course not," I said, a bit puzzled.

He opened the door to the freezer compartment. "Wow, you weren't kidding. You have a chicken franchise here! Kentucky Fried doesn't hold a candle to you."

We both laughed. "I *told* you my freezer is full of chicken. That's what you'll get when you come for dinner!"

CHAPTER 20

BOB AND I BEGAN DATING STEADILY. He made my heart sing, but I never expected to marry him. At the time, Jewish girls were expected to marry Jewish guys. When I told my parents I was dating someone who wasn't, my mom said, "It's a stage some girls go through. Several of my friends had a Gentile boyfriend before they settled down with someone Jewish."

The truth was, she and Dad were worried. I was twenty-six, and most of their friends' daughters my age were already married.

The trend in the Sixties was to marry right after college. They hoped I'd move on quickly.

I bought their message. In the end, I'd marry a *landsman*, I thought. So I didn't analyze whether Bob was good marriage material as I had with every other guy I'd dated. I felt freer to relax and get to know him. As a result, we formed a deep friendship as well as a romantic connection.

He had a wonderful sense of humor. His wit was clever, often a play on words, and we laughed a lot together. After we'd been dating for a few months, I invited my friend Madeline and her fiancé to a chicken dinner with me and Bob at my apartment. We had a great time, and Bob displayed his humorous side. "I never realized what a great sense of *humor* he has," she told me afterwards.

"He's funny when you get to know him," I said. It became my mantra whenever he said something that made me laugh.

The first summer we were together he said, "How'd you like to go to Maine for a week?"

"I'd love to," I said, though I felt some trepidation because of what my parents would think. I didn't lie when they asked if I was going with him. They were not pleased.

I was also not super comfortable as a single woman traveling with a boyfriend. I had worried about running into someone I knew.

We drove up the coast, spending time in Ogunquit, Boothbay Harbor, Bar Harbor, and Acadia National Park. Neither of us had been there before, and we loved the waves crashing against the immense rocks, the gulls flying around us and calling to each other as they swooped to grab food, the fishing boats coming in and out of the harbor, the fresh salty air.

We were charmed by the Down East Mainers' way of speaking, with many sentences ending in *ayah,* followed by a slight sucking in of breath. Bob was great with dialects and did a perfect imitation.

He had gone fishing often when he was growing up. On weekends, he and his cousin Vinny had headed for one of the nearby ponds in southwestern Connecticut to cast spinning rods from a rowboat. When I was growing up in New Jersey, my family sometimes took a day trip to the shore, rented an outboard motorboat, and fished for blues or stripers. Our childhood experiences had thus instilled in both of us an enjoyment of the sport.

"For me, it's the mystery of not knowing what's below the surface," Bob said. "I also love the tranquility that comes along with freshwater fishing."

In Maine, we enjoyed walking along the docks when the fishing boats were returning with the catch of the day. He had packed two lightweight fishing rods and his tackle box, in case we had an opportunity to use them. He didn't like party boats, preferring to fish from shore or from a small outboard—as I had done with my family.

We also discovered the tastes and smells of down-home Maine cooking: the best New England clam chowder, fresh-from-the-oven blueberry pie made with native Maine blueberries, chunks of lobster on toasted hot dog rolls dripping with butter, meaty and fresh fried clams, and whole steamed lobster served within two hours of being unloaded from a fisherman's lobster pot—accompanied by a roasted ear of corn.

Our best fishing moment occurred in front of an inn in Boothbay Harbor, where we were staying. It faced a narrow inlet, and we fished from the dock. As soon as we lowered our lines, using shiners as bait, snappers grabbed them.

We couldn't pull them in fast enough. Once they were caught, we released them. We could have been catching the same one over and over, but the schools of fish swarming around our lines were evidence that, most of the time, they were new catches.

Just south of Bar Harbor, we entered Acadia National Park, the *pièce de resistance* of the trip, located on Mount Desert Island and several smaller ones. I fell in love with walks along the craggy rocks at sea level and high above. In some spots, the waves crashed against the shore, particularly at Thunder Hole, where you could walk right to the edge of the rocks, feel the pounding of the water, and get drenched by gigantic bursts of spray.

Driving there and back in a rented Mercury coupe, we listened to the latest pop songs on the car radio. I associate Neil Diamond's "Sweet Caroline" most with that trip.

I WAS STILL SEEING NOHMIE MYERS when I started dating Bob. I had told her more than once that I really liked him but didn't see myself marrying him because he wasn't Jewish. I knew by then that he loved me, and he had talked about marriage.

"You're not being fair to him if you *know* you won't marry him," she said. "At some point soon, you need to tell him."

"But I enjoy being with him."

Then everything changed. I was having dinner with him at his apartment on East Eighty-fifth early in October—two years after our first date—when he again brought up the subject of marriage. "I love you, and I want to marry you," he said simply.

"I love you, too, but I just don't know. . . ."

After dinner, I hailed a cab in front of his apartment and was riding downtown to my own in heavy traffic when I had an epiphany: *I can't imagine spending the rest of my life without him.*

If it had been a movie, I would have told the cab driver to turn around, gone back to Bob's apartment, and declared my undying love. "Of course I want to marry you!" I'd have said as I ran into his arms.

Instead, I told him over the phone, and he came down to my apartment.

THE NEXT DAY, A SUNDAY, we phoned my parents to ask if we could stop by to say hello. They'd gotten to know Bob over the two years we'd been dating, but we were still nervous about their reaction to our marriage plans.

When we got there, we invited them to sit down in the living room. Bob and I sat next to each other on the couch; they each settled into a wing chair on either side of a small, antique wooden table against the wall to our right.

Bob asked them for my hand in marriage, and my father's and mother's eyes welled up as they gave their consent. Then Dad gazed at his future son-in-law intently and said, "You know, you're taking my most precious possession."

I looked at him and held back tears, thinking, *He really loves me.* Up until that point I had never been sure. He'd been so much more affectionate to Ruth. She was the one who often sat on his lap while I stood awkwardly at his side.

I hugged and kissed both of them, and Bob shook my father's hand and hugged Mom. It's a moment I treasure.

They invited us to stay and have dinner with them. After talking about wedding plans, Mom asked, "Have you talked about how you'll raise your children?"

Once I knew I wanted to marry Bob, I realized how important it was to me that we have a Jewish home and raise our children Jewish. I'd told him that.

"That's fine with me," he'd said without hesitation.

When Mom asked the question, Bob reassured her. "I'm very comfortable having a Jewish home if that's what Judy wants."

AT OUR WEDDING FOUR MONTHS LATER, Dad looked pale and gaunt, but he had a great time and smiled broadly. I worried about him during our honeymoon in St. Thomas. He was failing, and I knew he didn't have long to live. He died later that year at fifty-seven.

It's odd what one remembers after a parent dies. We sat *shiva* with my mother, and when one of Dad's friends paid a call, he pulled out pictures of his grandchildren and boasted in great detail about their talents.

How insensitive you are, I thought. *My father's dead and will never know his grandchildren.*

I returned to work a week later. My co-workers had sent a card, but only one said anything to me after I got back. Don, a writer in the Long Lines news division, stopped me when we passed in the hall. "So sorry to hear about your father. My deepest sympathy."

"Thanks, Don, I appreciate your condolences." I meant it.

I felt hurt and lonely after my dad died. Half of our immediate family was gone. I missed him terribly.

The opportunity to talk honestly with my father about his illness was also gone. I felt some consolation in knowing deep down that he'd probably been aware of his prognosis and had chosen not to talk about it. I also never told him how much I loved him. I like to think he knew that, too.

CHAPTER 21

TWO YEARS INTO OUR MARRIAGE, Bob and I decided to start a family. Before getting married, we'd each expressed a desire for two children. We were confident I'd get pregnant right away.

"How would you feel if I quit my job?" I asked him. "It might be nice to have some free time before I become a mom."

I also wasn't happy by then at Long Lines. Managers in the public relations department believed copywriters should learn to handle a variety of assignments. After writing for *Long Lines*, the advertising department, and *Management Report*, I had been transferred to the news division.

It didn't suit me. My forte was *not* turning out copy quickly, a requirement in news. I needed time to develop a story.

"It's okay with me," Bob said. "Adelson and Eichinger is doing well. Go for it."

After being in the news division for four weeks, I told the manager, Herb Linnen, I was resigning. He was shocked. "I know you're not happy in News, but you don't have to leave."

"It's not that," I answered. "It's time for a change." I had been at AT&T Long Lines for six years.

He tried to dissuade me, but I remained firm.

Richard Burke, one of the newer *Long Lines* magazine writers, organized a farewell luncheon for me at one of the local restaurants, and my colleagues wished me well.

REALITY HIT A FEW MONTHS LATER. I didn't get pregnant right away. After trying for three months, I burst into tears. "I can't believe I might not have children," I sobbed.

Bob was more sanguine. "You're jumping the gun," he said. "Everything we've read and heard says it sometimes takes as long as a year."

I'd been twenty-eight, and Bob thirty-three, on our wedding day. After we'd been married a year, some family members and friends had begun asking if and when we planned to have kids. I wanted to say, "None of your business," but instead I assured them, "You'll be the first to know."

We decided to consult a fertility expert after six months without success. By then I was a basket case. In the privacy of our apartment, I broke down each time my period arrived, and Bob had to console me. However, we didn't reveal to our family that we'd been trying without success. We only told one couple, close friends who were also having difficulty conceiving.

I did some research, and a doctor affiliated with New York Hospital with offices on Park Avenue seemed to be the expert of choice. We had to wait several weeks to see him.

His office was in the East Seventies. When we walked in, we

saw the waiting room was almost completely full. Only a few single seats were available. One couple moved over so we could sit together. "Welcome to a whole new world," I whispered in Bob's ear.

We noticed that a number of people were holding paper bags on their laps—specimens of some sort. Later—when we were waiting to see the doctor with a paper bag of our own—we figured these specimens had probably been freshly collected semen, brought in so the doctor could insert it high in the woman's cervix to increase the chances of her egg becoming fertilized.

Forty-five minutes later, we were ushered into his office. He was a handsome man in his mid-forties with touches of gray in his dark brown hair. He had an aura of self-confidence that was comforting and off-putting at the same time.

His handshake was weak, but I had found that to be the case with other doctors. *Maybe he's also a surgeon trying to protect his hands.*

He sat down at his desk and leaned back in his chair, clasping his hands behind his head. It wouldn't have surprised me if he had put his feet on the desk, but he didn't.

"So what's going on?" he asked.

"We've been trying to get pregnant for seven months," I said. "Because we're in our thirties—Bob's thirty-six, and I'm thirty-one, we thought it was time to see you."

"If there's a problem, we'll try to find it," he said.

"What's your success rate?" Bob asked.

"Pretty good. You've come to the right place."

Our journey into the world of infertility began. During that first visit, the doctor reviewed my gynecological history, gave me a physical exam, and drew blood to determine my hormone levels.

He also took a sample of my cervical fluid and looked at it under a microscope. "I see a few white cells," he said, "but not enough to cause the problem."

He told Bob he needed to see a urologist who would do a semen analysis to determine his sperm count and make sure that nothing else was going on at his end that needed to be addressed.

I was the major test taker. At the end of our initial visit, the staff scheduled several appointments for me. During the next two weeks, I had an ultrasound to check the condition of my ovaries and uterus, an x-ray of my fallopian tubes to rule out any blockage, and an endometrial biopsy to make sure the lining of my uterus was normal.

All the initial tests were normal. The next step was for me to begin charting my basal body temperature (BBT) every month.

To accurately record it, I needed to wake up at the same time every morning, immediately take my temperature, and enter it on a chart. When I ovulated, my BBT would rise and remain higher for the rest of the cycle.

I began a new BBT chart on the first day of my menstrual cycle and continued through the last day before beginning a new one. Most women who are regular have a twenty-eight-day cycle and ovulate after fourteen. The best time for sperm to fertilize the egg is twenty-four hours after ovulation. My cycle was very irregular. It could last for as little as twenty-six days or as long as thirty-eight. Because of this, I had no idea when I ovulated. By charting my BBT, I'd know when my egg would be most receptive.

The first time I charted my temperature, it remained low for twenty-one days. On day twenty-two, it rose almost a full degree. It was early morning on a work day, and Bob was still fast asleep.

He was on his side facing away from me. "Sweetheart," I said softly in his ear. "My temperature jumped this morning. I think I'm ovulating."

"Whaa . . . ?" He answered from some place far away.

"We need to have sex before you go to work."

He rolled over and looked at me with disbelief. "You mean *now*?"

I nodded.

It was not what anyone would have called "lovemaking." I think of it still as "baby making."

A FEW MORE MONTHS PASSED WITHOUT SUCCESS. The doctor suggested we try artificial insemination. In our case, it meant me bringing to the office a freshly collected sample, and having the doctor insert it high up into my cervix using something resembling a turkey baster. We did this for a couple of months without success. He analyzed my cervical mucus again and told us he still saw a few white cells.

"Could that be causing the problem?" Bob asked.

"No. If the engine of your car is broken, you can't fix it by changing a tire."

We looked at each other, uncertain of what he was saying.

Additional tests took place. One was a postcoital test after ovulation to make sure my cervical fluid was welcoming to Bob's sperm. After sex in the morning, I had to go to the doctor's office so he could take a sample and analyze it.

We met in his office soon afterward, and he gave us some bad news. "Your cervical fluid is rejecting Bob's sperm. It's as if you're allergic to each other."

". . .What do we do about it?"

"Bob needs to use a condom for a few months, and we'll test you again. Sometimes eliminating contact for a period of time changes the situation."

"This is crazy," I said to Bob afterward, holding back tears. We'd stopped at a coffee shop before heading to our apartment and sat opposite each other at a small table next to the window. I ordered a decaf cappuccino with a sprinkle of cinnamon and Bob a regular coffee. "We want to have a baby, and we need to use a condom that prevents me from getting pregnant? *What's wrong with this picture?*" I began to cry, which happened very frequently during that time.

Bob reached across to squeeze my hand. "Let's try it. Maybe it'll do the trick."

Our cups arrived. I sipped the hot coffee topped with foamy milk, and it felt soothing.

WE USED CONDOMS FOR SEVERAL MONTHS. Then one day I said to Bob, "Let's get a second opinion."

A friend suggested I talk to her gynecologist and obstetrician, Dr. William Walden. She described him as a doctor of the "old school" in the best sense of the phrase. "He takes his time, and he gives you his complete attention. When you go into labor, he's with you from the moment you get to the hospital until your baby is delivered."

If I ever get pregnant, I thought, I'd like that kind of a doctor. Most obstetricians had group practices. You never knew which doctor would be delivering your baby, and he or she often didn't arrive until shortly before you were wheeled into the delivery room.

I MET WITH DR. WALDEN LATER THAT WEEK. His office exuded an atmosphere completely different from what we'd been used to at the infertility specialist's office. The waiting room was much smaller, and only one other patient was there. Dr. Walden's wife was the receptionist, and very warm and welcoming. I was seeking a referral to an infertility specialist, so I didn't need an exam.

As I followed her to his office, I glanced into an empty examining room. On one wall I saw many snapshots of smiling babies. I found out later that he had delivered all of them. I sat in one of the two black leather chairs opposite the doctor's desk. Soon he walked in and closed the door behind him. He was soft-spoken, with a ready smile. He gave me a firm handshake. I immediately noticed his hair. He was wearing a jet black toupee. Despite the hairpiece, I liked him.

I told him the story and gave him a rundown of the tests and procedures we'd had. He suggested we see Dr. Gerson Weiss, a fertility specialist at New York University Medical Center. "We became good friends in medical school," he said, "and he has helped several of my patients."

The following week, we met Dr. Weiss. He was around five foot eight, stocky, and had a ruddy complexion, sandy-colored curly hair, and a full beard. He ushered us into his office and invited us to sit in the chairs opposite his modest wooden desk. Dark floor-to-ceiling wooden shelves behind the desk were filled with medical books. A large casement window to our left revealed an overcast sky.

After reviewing our history, he asked me to follow his nurse to an examining room. Bob waited in the reception area. I removed my clothes, put on the blue paper gown that had been placed on the exam table, and sat on the edge.

Soon, the doctor tapped on the door and entered. He gave me a thorough physical. Before finishing, he took a sample of my cervical fluid and looked at it under a microscope.

After I got dressed, we reconvened in his office. "Did the specialist you've been seeing ever say anything about finding white cells in your cervical mucus?"

"He said he saw a few, but that they weren't our main problem."

He pursed his lips. "The presence of white cells means you have an infection. You can't get pregnant until you clear it up."

He put me on tetracycline and told me to come back in thirty days. "Don't try to get pregnant while you're taking the medication, but once you've finished it, try again."

We were dumbfounded. It couldn't be that simple.

Thirty days later, we returned to his office. He took a sample of my cervical fluid. "Infection's gone," he said. The following month I became pregnant.

WE SIGNED UP FOR LAMAZE childbirth classes to learn a controlled breathing technique to cope with labor. It can help a prospective mother endure the discomfort and pain before and during delivery. The couple works together, with the husband learning the method, so he can coach his wife during her contractions.

The classes were held in New York Hospital, and we attended our first one at the end of my sixth month. We entered the hospital elevator with several other people. Bob and I stepped to the back, facing forward. On the next floor, our first infertility specialist got on. He stood facing us. The next floor was ours. When we got off,

I looked at him and smiled. I wanted him to remember me and see I was pregnant. Our eyes met, but he showed no sign of recognition.

Karen Irene Eichinger was born in January, 1976. We chose her first name because I liked it, and Bob didn't object. Her middle name was in memory of my father, Ira.

The day we brought her home from the hospital, it was bitter cold—one of the coldest days on record. A few days afterwards, the weather became a bit more temperate, so we bundled Karen up, put her in her carriage, and wheeled her along East Eighty-sixth Street, where we lived. As we walked, I looked at her snuggled peacefully under her blankets, got all choked up, and said to Bob, "I'd give my life for her."

WE WANTED OUR TWO CHILDREN to be at least three years apart. We were ready to begin trying to have our second baby three months after Karen turned two. However, I wanted to make sure the new baby didn't arrive on or near my sister's birthday in February. So we waited until June 1978 to stop using birth control. I became pregnant two months later.

Because I was thirty-six then and Bob forty-one, we decided that I'd undergo amniocentesis—a test used to determine certain genetic disorders, more prevalent in the fetus of a woman over thirty-five. It's performed between the fourteenth and sixteenth weeks of pregnancy and also determines the sex of the child.

When I had the test, Dr. Walden asked us if we wanted to know whether it was a boy or a girl. We said we weren't sure. I was at home when Dr. Walden's nurse called us with the results. "You're going to have a healthy male," she said.

It didn't register at first. I'd heard the word "healthy" and was thrilled. Then I realized she had told me the sex.

Bob and I decided not to let anyone know we were having a boy. I was superstitious. I didn't believe in baby showers before a child is born, and I wasn't comfortable revealing the sex for the same reason.

I was happy it was going to be a boy for two reasons: I wanted to have the experience of raising a son as well as a daughter, and I was afraid of repeating the pattern of having two girls, fearing the younger one would get sick just like Ruth did.

One Sunday when I was seven months pregnant, my mother and Bob's father and stepmother visited us. They started talking about the sex of their expected grandchild.

"I hope it's a boy," Elizabeth said. "It would be nice to have one of each."

"I hope it's a girl," my mother countered. "I like little girls."

Bob and I smiled at each other.

Daniel Jacob Eichinger arrived in April 1979. I had loved the name Daniel all my life, so I was set on his first name. Since Karen's middle name was for my father, we decided that Daniel's middle name would be Jacob, Bob's father's name. My mother was unhappy we hadn't named him after Ruth until she learned from a friend that, in the Jewish religion, a new baby is not named for a child who died young.

Before Daniel was born, I was concerned about not loving him as much as Karen. But when I saw him for the first time, I discovered what all parents with more than one child know: Our capacity to love each of our children is limitless.

Part Two

CHAPTER 22

I
T WAS AN ORDINARY SATURDAY—a brisk, clear fall day, the red, gold, and orange leaves on the trees shimmering in the brilliant sunlight.

We had moved to Teaneck, New Jersey, in the spring of 1980—a town known for those trees. It was the majestic, towering oak on the left side of the three-bedroom colonial we lived in that had beckoned to Bob when we were house hunting. It was one of eleven trees on the half-acre—along with three maples, two gigantic twin fir, two pines, one cedar, and two birches.

Mrs. Baumgart, a widow who sold us the house, had prided herself on keeping every room in pristine condition. The real estate agent had told us the owner had refused to sell to a previous couple because the wife had run her finger over the top of a bedroom door to test for dust.

By contrast, Mrs. Baumgart hadn't done much with the property surrounding the house. The trees needed pruning, and we hired a service to do this soon after we moved in. It was a safety issue.

They looked even more beautiful when they were trimmed. After living in an apartment for almost ten years, we reveled in our "estate."

Towards evening on that ordinary Saturday, Bob and I went to see *Ordinary People,* which was playing at the movie theater on Cedar Lane—the main artery running through downtown Teaneck. We hired Michelle, the teenager who lived across the street, to stay with our two children.

"I think the kids loved your dinner as much as I did," I said as we pulled out of the driveway. Bob gets great pleasure out of cooking and usually cooks on weekends. That evening he'd made chicken paprikash with spaetzle—a pasta favored by Hungarians like his mother. It was one of the dishes he grew up with. We'd all cleaned our plates; Karen had even sucked on the bones. Accompanying the main course had come a delicious salad with all the fixings and Bob's homemade vinaigrette.

"What should we have for dinner tomorrow?" he asked.

"I'm too full to think about it right now," I said. "Call me at lunch time and I'll tell you."

That was a joke between us. When I worked at Long Lines, a middle-aged man named John on the magazine's production staff had called his wife every day just before lunch to find out what she was making for dinner. "What're we having?" he'd ask. That way he'd know what *not* to eat for lunch.

We continued our easy banter as we drove the two miles to Cedar Lane and parked in the main municipal parking around the corner.

I didn't know much about the movie, only that it was Robert Redford's directorial debut, had an all-star cast, and had received excellent reviews.

The theater was crowded, but we were able to get two seats on the aisle fairly close to the screen, where we liked to sit. We settled in our seats in time to see the first of several previews. Then the movie began.

As I watched, the internal agony the main character, Conrad Jarrett (Timothy Hutton), is going through felt achingly familiar. Shortly after the movie begins, the viewer finds out that Conrad's older brother, Buck, died in a boating accident. Both were sailing together, a storm came up, the sailboat capsized, and only Conrad survived.

We also find out that, not too long after this tragedy, Conrad slashed his wrists and spent four months in a psychiatric hospital. He's just returned home and is still dealing with those issues.

As I sat next to Bob in the darkened theater, my face and body began to sweat. I felt a shock of recognition. Although the particulars were different, I knew what Conrad was feeling—or rather *not* feeling.

I had entered the same unchartered territory after Ruth's death.

I know why you're out of control, I told Conrad silently. *You've lost your brother and you're tortured that you survived.*

And in that darkened theater, I moved from being a detached observer to an active participant in Conrad's story. I was completely invested in what he would do next.

No one in the movie understands why Conrad is acting the way he is. He can't *connect* with anyone—especially his mother, and to a lesser extent his father. His friends don't get it, his swimming coach doesn't get it, and most of all *he* doesn't get it.

Conrad has the hardest time dealing with his mother, Beth

(Mary Tyler Moore). She acts cold and unfeeling toward him. He is bewildered by her behavior, and when he tries clumsily to reach out to her, she cuts him off. There is a wall around her. His father (Donald Sutherland) is also miffed. He wants to help resolve the schism, but he doesn't know how.

Another shock of recognition shot through my body as I watched these scenes of Conrad with his parents. While they weren't the same as mine, there were similarities.

When Ruth died, I felt I had lost my parents as well. They were consumed by grief and shut me out emotionally. Two decades later, my mother still couldn't get past that grief to understand mine. I felt guilty that I didn't know how to reach out to her and angry that she couldn't reach out to me.

Like Conrad's father, mine was extremely stoic and never expressed his own sorrow. It seemed as if he wanted me to be "okay," so I could give my mother comfort. I dealt with all this by tamping down my feelings as much as possible. I was so afraid of all hell breaking loose if I confronted them.

Many of Conrad's other contacts felt familiar, too. One is with his best friend. Conrad has pushed his friends away. At one point, his closest one jumps into the front seat of the car after school just as Conrad is starting the engine.

"Wanna talk?"

Conrad doesn't say anything.

". . . What is it with you? Why do you want to be in this alone?"

No answer.

"You know, I miss him, too," the friend says. "The three of us were best friends."

Finally Conrad speaks. "I can't. It hurts too much to be around you."

I felt my face flushing in the dark. I remembered what one of my high school friends had told me shortly after Ruth died. "I had no idea Ruth was so sick. It must have been so hard to deal with. If you had opened up to me, I could have been there for you."

It hurt too much to tell you, I had said to myself.

There was another friend I didn't confide in. Her brother was severely disabled developmentally. She never talked about him and how his condition was affecting her life. It hit me that she and I had a lot in common but never said a word to each other. How weird that seems now, I thought.

My eyes remained glued to the big screen. I was hungry for more of Conrad's story. Embedded in it were the clues to my own, and I needed to know how his would be resolved.

Conrad has been seeing Dr. Berger, a therapist, played beautifully by Judd Hirsch, but has resisted discussing his feelings with Berger—which is how he addresses him. Conrad's defenses come crashing down when he finds out his closest friend from the psychiatric hospital has killed herself. It is the middle of the night, and Conrad's parents are out of town. Sobbing, he desperately calls Berger, who tells him to meet him at his office.

Through gentle probing, Berger finds out about the suicide.

"I could have done something," Conrad says. "Why do things happen? It isn't fair. You do just one wrong thing . . . " His voice tapers off.

"What was the wrong thing you did?" Berger asks.

Conrad stops talking for a moment. "I hung on—stayed with the boat."

"Exactly. You can live with that, can't you?"

"I'm scared."

"Feelings are scary, sometimes painful. If you can't feel pain, you can't feel anything else. You're here, and you're alive."

"It doesn't feel good."

"It *is good, believe me.*"

"How do you know?"

"Because I am your friend."

"Are you really my friend?"

"I am. Count on it."

Berger hugs him tightly as Conrad throws his arms around the therapist and sobs onto his shoulder. It is the movie's cathartic moment, and in that darkened theater I cried with Conrad for his loss and for my own.

As I watched them embrace, I felt pangs of jealousy. I wanted Berger to wrap his arms around *me* and tell me he was *my* friend. I wanted a safe place where *I* could explore all the feelings I had about Ruth and her death that I hadn't dealt with.

Why do I get so angry whenever her name is mentioned? Why can't I speak her name? Why can't I tell people I had a sister when they ask me?

I need to find my own Berger, I said to myself.

I felt like a wet dish rag when the movie ended. I had cried more tears into more tissues in those two hours than I had in the last twenty years since Ruth's death.

My eyes were swollen, and my nose felt red and raw. As we walked up the aisle in the dimly lit theater, I prayed I wouldn't run into anyone I knew.

When Bob and I hit the street, I was numb. Somehow I expected him to know what an emotional roller coaster I'd been on while watching the movie. Surely he had noticed me reach into my bag several times for tissues. But his first comments were jarring. "I don't know what the big deal is about the movie," he said. As we walked to the street corner, past a couple of storefront restaurants, a closed framing store, and a shuttered women's boutique, he went on to criticize aspects of the film's production and direction.

I was so drained by the movie's emotional power, and so angry at him for not understanding why it touched me so deeply, that I couldn't speak.

"Are you telling me," I finally managed to ask, "you weren't moved by the story?"

"It was cliché."

I started to cry. "I thought it was an *incredible* movie," I said through my tears. I started choking on my words as the tears continued. I was furious that he didn't get it. "You have no *feelings!*" I lashed out. "How could you not understand what he was *going* through?"

He started to respond and then thought better of it. We crossed the street, reached the parking lot, got in the car, and rode the short distance home in silence.

It was only after we had gotten to the house, paid the babysitter, and watched as she crossed the street and entered her house that I began to see things from Bob's point of view.

How *could* he have understood? He was an only child. He had no idea what it was like to lose a brother or sister.

I wanted him to read my mind, feel my pain, comfort me, and console me. How could he do that if I couldn't recognize and express it to myself?

For twenty years I had closed off the part of me that needed to grasp my feelings before I could explain them to anyone else—including the person I was closest to.

Before going to bed, we sat down in the living room. I was much calmer at that point and able to tell him about the feelings the movie had stirred up. He is the love of my life and a very giving person. But he is incapable of reading my mind. "I need professional help," I told him. He agreed.

Ordinary People opened the door. I knew I was hurting in every fiber of my body, and I didn't know how to deal with it. My sister had died decades before. It was time to confront the pain and work through it.

CHAPTER 23

THERE WERE FIVE WOMEN, including me, sitting in the waiting area of a small, two-story professional building off County Road in Cresskill, New Jersey. We had never met and were about to begin our first group therapy session. I had butterflies in my stomach and was working hard to control my anxiety.

The couch and two of the chairs were covered in a warm, burnt orange corduroy. There were three additional plastic chairs in neutral colors that looked hard and forbidding but were surprisingly comfortable.

Two of us were on the couch, two on chairs, and one on the carpeted stairs that led to the second floor. The overhead lighting was subdued. We occasionally glanced at one another other but didn't say anything.

AFTER LIVING IN TEANECK for several months, I had finally realized I needed psychological help. When I was seeing Nohmie Myers in New York, she'd suggested group therapy, but I'd rejected the idea.

Now, I knew it was what I needed to help me build closer relationships with women in my community.

It wasn't a new problem. As a stay-at-home mother of a toddler in Manhattan, I hadn't established close friendships with any of the other mothers I knew. Elsie, with whom I'd shared a hospital room when our daughters were born, lived nearby. We would sometimes get together and remained casual acquaintances.

I had literally bumped into Alice, whom I'd met a few years before in an art class, when we were pushing our baby carriages along Second Avenue on the Upper East Side. We had no idea we'd each given birth to a baby girl, and it rekindled our relationship. We'd sometimes arranged playdates for our daughters. But I had remained guarded.

Most mornings I wheeled my carriage to Carl Schurz Park on the East River—two blocks from our one-bedroom apartment on East Eighty-sixth—and sat on a bench, with other new mothers, in one of the shady sitting areas. We compared notes about our children's behavior, growth, sleep patterns, and eating habits. But I didn't get to know any of them well.

After leaving the park, I'd shop for food, go home, and put Karen down for a nap. Our TV was in the living room, and I'd turn it on and listen to soap operas while I prepared dinner in the kitchen.

Every day, I waited for Bob to return from work to take over handling the demands of an active toddler.

After Daniel was born three years later, we had moved into a two-bedroom apartment on a higher floor in the same building. When he was several months old and Karen almost four, we'd started talking about moving to the suburbs. Our rental building was going co-op, and Karen was approaching school age. It was hard to get kids into one of the few public schools that were highly rated, and private schools were very expensive and not what we wanted philosophically for our kids.

I had certain prejudices about the suburbs, though, and was skeptical about moving out of the city. In my mind, suburbanites were superficial. Their cultural tastes were low- brow and, for the most part, uninteresting.

"Suburban women think primarily about their clothes and spend most of their time taking care of their kids and going to lunch with their friends," I said more than once.

My stereotypical suburban dad worked hard all day, had dinner with his family, read the paper or watched TV, and went to bed.

The funny thing was that my own family, when I was growing up, hadn't fit that picture. My parents had a rich cultural and social life in the suburbs—despite my sister being seriously ill. My mother was a stay-at-home mom, but she was also a Girl Scout leader, a Red Cross volunteer, and very active in the schools. She and my father periodically drove into the City to see a Broadway show. Mom was very involved in my sister's care, but whenever possible she accompanied my father on business trips—particularly to an annual packaging convention in Chicago.

Dad's business was in Hillside, New Jersey-—twenty minutes from our house. We ate dinner soon after he came home from work. Afterwards, he would take a short power nap and head off to a meeting of one of the organizations in which he was active. He occupied leadership positions in the synagogue, the Masonic lodge, and various community groups.

Mom and Dad developed a large network of friends through the various organizations in which they were active. They would get together at another couple's house on Saturday evenings or host parties characterized by a lot of laughter and camaraderie. Ruth and I used to sit at the top of the stairs and listen to what was going on.

One party I remember in particular was a Mad Hatter event. Guests were required to wear a funny hat—the more outlandish, the better. My dad made his signature dish, a baked barbecue steak that took all day to prepare. Their friends said it melted in their mouths. I have the recipe, handed down, but Bob and I have never made it. Eating styles have changed, and we eat meat that's much leaner and requires less preparation.

When Bob and I began looking for a house, we started in Westchester, but most of the houses in our price range were small and didn't have garages. So we set our sights on northern New Jersey, where I'd grown up. We looked at communities that had good school systems and offered Bob a fairly easy commute to his studio in mid-town Manhattan.

Ian, a fellow who sublet space from Bob, invited us to brunch at his house in Teaneck. "Our daughters have had only positive experiences in the township schools," he said, and suggested we consider his community.

When I got out of our car after Bob parked in front of Ian's house, I had an immediate gut reaction. "I can't explain it," I said to him, "but I feel at home here."

The trees that lined the street were stately and beautiful, and I liked the mix of house styles. There were also sidewalks, which was important to us. We wanted our kids to be able to ride their scooters or walk to neighbors' houses without having to go into the street.

The following weekend, a real estate agent took us to see several available houses—including the one we bought. It was the last one she showed us. We had no idea where we were in relation to Ian's house, but we called him and asked him to come over to check it out. Bob gave him the address.

"Hey, dude," Ian said, "we're on the same street a block and a half away. I'll be there in two minutes."

That was in the late Fall of 1979. We moved in the following Spring.

Being a mother of two young children in my new community was, for me, very isolating. A couple of Manhattan friends had given us names of people to contact after we moved in. I remember one in particular. When I called her, she was very warm and welcoming, and invited us to a backyard barbecue she was hosting that Sunday. My anxiety took over, though, and I politely declined.

Shortly after we moved in, someone told me about a summer playgroup that was being formed by mothers of four-year-olds. Two elementary school teachers were going to run it, and the playgroup would move every three days from one house to the next. The number of kids would be limited to fifteen, and all the activities would take place in each home's backyard unless it was raining. The host mother was responsible for providing wholesome snacks and drinks.

I signed up Karen and joined a car pool with other participants who lived near us. I met many women through the playgroup and developed casual relationships with a number of them.

That summer, we had applied for, and were accepted as weekday members of, the Teaneck Swim Club. A number of families with children in the playgroup had already joined.

At the pool, I'd hung out with some of the mothers from the summer play group while our kids splashed in the water. But, once again, the relationships I developed had been superficial.

The summer passed, and I still hadn't gotten serious about finding a therapy group. Then, in the Fall, I'd seen *Ordinary People*, and it had become an imperative.

I invited one of Karen's kindergarten classmates to come over for a play date. I didn't know her mother well, but I felt I could confide in her. Once the kids ran off to the playroom behind our kitchen, she and I chatted in the foyer. I swallowed hard and got up the courage to ask her the question I'd been practicing in my mind for days.

"Do you—-d'you know any therapists who do group therapy?"

"My husband has been seeing a psychiatrist in Tenafly, and he really likes her," she said. "She only sees patients individually, but maybe she can recommend someone. I'll call you with her phone number."

She got back to me with the number later that day, and I called. The doctor sounded very nice. "My friend and colleague, Harriet Copeland, is starting a therapy group shortly. I've known her a long time, and I recommend her very highly."

She gave me her number, and I called her before I had time to change my mind.

Mrs. Copeland—she asked me to call her Harriet—and I chatted for a few minutes on the phone, and scheduled an appointment for me to meet with her in her office. She wanted to get acquainted, she said, before the group began.

I liked her voice. It was mellow and soothing. She usually saw patients in her Cresskill office but asked me to come to her Fair

Lawn home office for an assessment.

There was no waiting area there. The entrance was on the side of the house off the driveway. I knocked on the door. "Come in," Harriet said.

The office was small—perhaps nine feet by eleven. Harriet sat next to a wooden desk, and I took the chair facing her. Behind the desk was a brown leather love seat with colorful throw pillows, above which, through a window, I could see sun-dappled leaves dancing in the breeze.

On the floor lay a multi-color area rug, and there were a small table and chair against the wall opposite the desk. Several family pictures hung above them. Behind my chair, a glass-paneled door led to the rest of the house. Everything was done in warm colors, and the room was welcoming and cozy.

One drawback: There was a strong smell of cigarette smoke. I found out quickly that Harriet was a chain smoker. She didn't smoke during our session, but it was obvious, from the ashtrays and smell in the air that she, and probably other patients, did.

She was slightly unkempt, with short brown hair, a sallow complexion, and thick eyeglasses. But she was very pleasant and made me feel comfortable. I sat down, we looked at each other for a couple of minutes, and then she spoke.

"So tell me about yourself."

"I have a wonderful husband and two wonderful kids," I said, "but I'm very lonely. I don't have any close friends, and I depend on my husband to fill all my needs."

I told her that seeing *Ordinary People* had stirred up a lot of unresolved feelings connected with the death of my sister. "My difficulty in forming close relationships may stem from that.

"I was proud of being very independent when I was growing up, but in retrospect I don't think that was such a good thing. . . . Mom would accuse me of being a very cold person when she got angry at me, and I took that message to heart."

Harriet was very empathetic. The fifty minutes flew by.

At the end of the session, she said, "I think group therapy will be very beneficial for you. We'll start with five women and possibly add some men in the future."

I felt a wave of panic. Group therapy seemed like a great idea in theory, but the reality terrified me. How could my needs be met when there would be four others vying for her attention? My heart was racing, but I kept my fears to myself.

We'd meet on Wednesday evenings in Cresskill beginning the following week.

CHAPTER 24

ARRIET CAME OUT OF HER OFFICE on the second floor and paused at the head of the stairs. All five of us looked up. "Please, come with me," she said.

We walked up the short flight and followed her down a carpeted hall and into the office. There were just enough chairs for all of us. They were arranged in an informal circle. Harriet's wooden desk was against the wall to the left of the door, and she had swiveled the seat of her chair so it faced into the room. Her colleague, John Burn—who was going to assist her—sat opposite the door on the far side of the room. He was a few years older than Harriet, and he had a ruddy complexion and thinning brown hair. He was stocky, his face kind, his earnest eyes blue.

Sandy chose the sling-back chair between Harriet and the door, and Gina and I shared the love seat against the wall. Sunny settled into the chair on Harriet's left; Sue Ann sat between Sunny and John.

Harriet introduced John, who spoke for a couple of minutes

about his counseling background. Then she invited each of us to say something about ourselves and what had brought us.

Sandy, who spoke first, was an early-childhood education teacher in her early thirties with a full head of light brown, naturally curly hair that fell loosely around her face. She had a charming grin that revealed top incisors slightly longer than the rest of her teeth. She was in jeans, a T-shirt, a jacket, and sneakers. She also seemed somewhat shy.

"My romantic relationships always go sour after a few months," she began. She looked down at the floor or at Harriet when she began. "Something always goes wrong. . . . I want to get married and have kids. I'm on the other side of thirty and not getting any younger," she concluded in frustration.

Sue Ann was also in her early thirties, had short, wavy dark brown hair, and was slightly overweight. She wore a simple cotton skirt, blouse, and flats. She smiled when she talked, even when she was describing something unpleasant. A nurse, she loved to play the piano. "My dream is to buy a used upright and give music lessons," she said. "Right now I don't make that much money so it's out of the question."

She seemed sweet but sometimes tittered at the end of a sentence. "Every man I've dated turned out to be out of the norm in some way," she continued. "I can never pick up the signals that they're weird."

Gina, in her mid-thirties, sat next to me. She was a tall, big-boned woman with shoulder-length hair, black and wavy, and perfectly manicured fingernails. An executive secretary at a company in downtown Manhattan, she looked professional in a dark, pretty skirt, a blouse, and low patent leather heels; she had a patent bag, too.

I immediately liked her and also felt a special kinship: Her face had pockmarks, and I'd had severe acne when I was growing up, had suffered from it psychologically and physically.

I had once overheard my aunt say to my mother, "If Judy didn't have acne, she'd be very pretty."

Gina also spoke about finding suitable male companionship. "The only long-term relationship I've had was with one of the managers where I work," she said. "He made me feel good as a person but broke up with me after two years when the company transferred him to another part of the country." She hadn't dated anyone seriously in the several years since.

The fourth member of the group was Sunny, who was plump, blond, and wore too much perfume. She had on black slacks and a pink angora sweater. She was in an unhealthy relationship and didn't know how to end it.

I was very nervous as I waited to talk. Finally, all eyes turned toward me.

"I'm fortunate to be married to a wonderful man who's my best friend," I said, "but I don't have any other close friends. My biggest problem is that I can't connect with my feelings, particularly my anger. My sister was sick her whole life and died when we were teenagers. I think that experience has a lot to do with why I can't get close to people."

I didn't know how group therapy was going to work for me. I was used to individual sessions that had involved just me and the therapist. We'd spend the allotted time discussing my problems and possible solutions. In group I'd have to vie with four other individuals for the therapist's attention.

Group therapy works when you trust the therapist and the

other participants to keep private whatever is said. It took a while for me and the others to feel this trust.

One of the first things John helped me understand was that whatever I was feeling was okay. That included anger and rage toward my sister and my parents, which I hadn't ever recognized.

"You have a right to feel what you feel," he said. "What you do with that feeling is another story."

A few weeks after group began, Bob and I were having dinner at a restaurant with another couple, and he made a comment about me in front of them that I felt was demeaning. I was seething, but I kept my anger in check until we got home. Then I let him have it. "How *dare* you belittle me in front of other people!" I screamed. "If you have a problem with me, tell me in *private*."

I continued screaming at the top of my lungs until I was hoarse. I'd fixed my hands indignantly on my hips the whole time.

He stared at me as if I were a lunatic. "You're right," he finally said quietly. "I shouldn't have said what I did. But your screaming doesn't help."

I felt good that I was able to voice my anger, but I needed to do it without screaming my lungs out.

ONE DAY IN GROUP, I came to the shocking realization that I was mirroring my mother's behavior. When she became angry at me while I was growing up, *she* had screamed at *me*. In discussing my childhood in group, I felt the jolt of this revelation. What's more, screaming had been the norm when *she* was growing up.

With each passing week, I began to express more of how I felt. I became more aware of my anger, and understood that I had as much a right to be angry as anyone else. It took a long time to get there, and it wasn't easy sailing.

A big piece of it was how angry I was at Ruth.

Why did *you have to die?* I wanted to know. *You were my champion, my playmate, my best friend and confidante, my ally in our family, and you deserted me.*

After Ruth died, I had felt a vulnerability that I'd never had before. If she could die young, so could I. My fear of airplanes didn't exist because my first flight after her death had been turbulent. I had felt even more vulnerable in a plane because I felt a total loss of control and knew fate could strike me, too.

As I began to express these feelings, I found I wasn't just angry, I was furious. The feelings had been locked inside me for more than twenty years, and I'd never wanted to face them. They weren't *nice* feelings, and having them made me a pretty horrible person, I thought.

They proved more complicated than just being angry at Ruth. Dealing with the anger I felt toward my parents was much more difficult, the feelings more toxic to identify or express.

Immediately after Ruth died, friends and family had begun gathering at our house. Their condolences had been directed toward my parents, even when they were speaking to me. "You need to be strong for your folks," one of their close friends had said to me.

Others had asked, "How are your parents doing?"

Not one person—not even my mother or father—had asked me how *I* was doing.

My parents quickly established The Ruth Gottscho Kidney Foundation in her memory. All their close friends rallied to the cause. They formed a board of directors and asked me to serve as a board member. I said yes but seethed with anger. They didn't realize how angry I was, or why.

The foundation raised a lot of money and helped many people with kidney disorders who lived in New Jersey. I dutifully attended meetings and approved motions, but I functioned like an automaton. I hated myself for being that way, too, and thought I was a terrible person.

"After Ruth died, what I wanted most was my parents' complete attention," I told the group. "The first thing they did was form a foundation in her memory. . . . Then they decided to give my sister's clothes to a needy Greek child who was Ruth's age. They found Alena through the organization Save the Children.

"On one of my father's business trips to Europe, they both went to Greece to meet her," I added. "From that point on, they called Alena 'our Greek daughter.'

"When I was twenty-four, my parents took my sixteen-year-old cousin, Linda, and the daughter of my father's British business representative, on a trip across the United States. I was working and couldn't go. I didn't realize at the time how resentful I was," I confessed.

As I began addressing these feelings, the others said they understood my resentment. Still, I became more and more uncomfortable. I began to have panic attacks again and grew deeply depressed. Until that moment, I hadn't understood how debilitating depression could be.

I lost my appetite and picked at my food. I rapidly became almost dysfunctional. Some mornings I couldn't get out of bed, and I missed days at work.

I called Harriet several times between group sessions, and talking to her helped at first. But soon I couldn't bounce back. She said I needed to take an anti-depressant.

"I don't believe in medication," I told her. "I don't like to take anything that isn't natural."

"You're feeling this way because you're making progress, and in the process you're stirring up some strong feelings," she said. "So you have a choice: Take the medication to help you move forward, or don't take it and stay where you are."

She was right. "Okay," I said.

Harriet referred me to Dr. Laura Odian, a psychiatrist with whom she worked, to prescribe an anti-depressant. I called and made an appointment to meet with her the following evening.

The next twenty-four hours were the hardest. I was trembling, crying, listless, and felt like I was going to die.

"I can't handle this," I said to Bob. "I'm going to end up in an institution."

"No, you're not."

". . . You think I'm going to get better?"

"Absolutely."

He said it with sincerity and conviction. His confidence helped calm me down.

As he drove me to Dr. Odian's office, I kept telling him how depressed I felt, and he kept reassuring me that everything would be okay.

The office was in the same building as Harriet's. It was smaller, but the furnishings were in similarly warm earth tones.

Dr. Odian was short and stout, and she wore her blond hair pulled back in a bun. She was several years older than I, very friendly, and spoke in a soft, calming manner. I sat on the small couch, and she settled into a chair across from me.

"Harriet filled me in about the issues you're dealing with," she said. "Tell me what's going on now and how you're feeling."

I described the anger I was getting in touch with and my ongoing struggle with panic attacks and depression. "I feel as if I've become *unhinged*," I said in despair.

She became thoughtful. "I'm going to prescribe Tofranil," she said. "It's been around a long time, and it's proven to treat panic attacks very well. The drug takes about four weeks to kick in," she explained. "You might experience some unpleasant side effects during the first few days, but they will subside. You may also feel your heart race, but that will also pass. If it bothers you, we can put you on Inderal for a short while."

She liked Tofranil better than some of the newer drugs, she said, because it caused fewer of the long-term side effects like significant weight gain and reduced libido.

She called in the prescription to our pharmacist so I could pick it up on the way home and begin taking it that evening.

I liked her a lot and sensed that the drug would help. All I had to do was get through the next few weeks.

We picked up the medication, I took it before bedtime, and went to sleep.

Around three a.m. I woke up with a terrible burning sensation at the top of my head. I nudged Bob.

"I don't know what to do," I said to my very sleepy husband. "I feel as if my scalp is on fire."

"I don't know what to tell you," he said. "Why don't you call Harriet."

I punched in Harriet's number. My brief conversation with her reassured me and made a big difference in my recovery.

"The burning sensation you feel is a side effect of the medication," she said. "It won't harm you, and it'll subside soon."

Her confidence that I'd be okay, that the medication wasn't harming me, calmed me down and helped me get back to sleep.

The following night, I had the same sensation, but it wasn't as severe. The third night, I hardly noticed it.

But my panic attacks and depression didn't begin to subside for more than three weeks. During that period, I somehow got myself to work and to group.

In group one Wednesday evening during this adjustment period, I was feeling very depressed and couldn't concentrate. I had also gotten very little sleep the night before. I was sitting there, but all I wanted to do was go home and get into bed. At one point, when another group member was talking, I interrupted to say, "Harriet, I'm feeling very tired and can't concentrate. Can I leave early?"

I expected her to be sympathetic and grant me permission to leave.

"No, you need to stay," she said. "It's important that you stick it out."

I was angry, and my face got red, but I knew she was right. I couldn't keep running away from situations that were uncomfortable. I stayed until the end and was able to walk out with the other members of the group, making small talk as we headed to the parking lot.

CHAPTER 25

When Karen was ten, she and her friend Bibi spent two weeks at Frost Valley YMCA Camp in the Catskill Mountains. It is the same facility that runs the kidney camp program sponsored by The Ruth Gottscho Kidney Foundation. Bob and I wanted Karen to attend Frost Valley because it is one of the best-run camps in the country and very popular with Teaneck families. Its philosophy, and the values it instills in campers, are very similar to those of Eagle Island, the Girl Scout camp I attended.

Frost Valley is spread over 5,000 beautiful acres in the heart of the Catskills, two hours from Teaneck. It is a mix of flat, grassy playing fields, shady hiking paths through woodlands, gurgling streams, and a pristine lake for swimming and boating. Rustic cabins are scattered over the rocky terrain above the main buildings. The air is sweet and clean, and beckons to anyone who loves the outdoors.

It was the first time Karen had gone to sleep-away camp. She hadn't been crazy about the idea. Getting a friend to go with her did the trick. Recalling how much I had loved my rustic experiences at Girl Scout camp, I was sure she would love Frost Valley once she was there, and want to return.

To get to camp, she took one of the chartered camp buses from northern New Jersey. We arranged to pick her up at the end of the session.

On the final day of camp, we showed up early. After parking the car, we ran into Frost Valley's CEO, Halbe Brown, who had approved the establishment of the kidney camp program eleven years before. The Ruth Gottscho Dialysis Center—paid for primarily by the foundation—occupied a small wing of the health center in Smith Lodge, just behind the welcome area where we were.

Central casting could not have chosen anyone more perfect for the role of CEO, both in looks and personality. He was a man in his fifties who wore green shorts and a yellow Frost Valley T-shirt. His face, legs, and arms were muscular and tan, a picture of health. He ran his fingers through thick curly hair and gave us a broad grin. He knew I was Eva's daughter, with whom he kept in close contact during the summer camp season.

"Hello! So good to see you," he said, extending his right hand and giving each of us a firm handshake. "Do you want to visit the dialysis center?"

"Sure," I said, although my throat tightened at the suggestion.

"I'll get one of our staff to walk you over."

I hadn't seen the center since it was built eleven years before. I wasn't crazy about seeing it again, but I felt I couldn't say no. Intellectually, I knew the kidney camp program was a resounding success. For the first time, kids with kidney disease could go to sleep-away camp because there was a dialysis center on site. Those with very low or no kidney function spent three hours a day three times a week connected to a dialysis machine. Kids with kidney transplants needed to stop by the unit daily to take anti-rejection medications. Others with chronic kidney disease, who didn't need dialysis or a kidney transplant, also needed to visit the unit to take medication and get checked by a nurse.

The center was staffed by a pediatric nephrologist and several pediatric nephrology nurses. Each summer, forty to fifty kids with kidney disease get to feel like normal kids and benefit from all that camp offers. They grow stronger physically and emotionally from the experience.

Nonetheless, I harbored a resentment toward the place. . . but I couldn't say no.

A lovely young staff member came to take us there. Bob and Halbe strode off, and the staff member and I followed.

"The dialysis center is *amazing*," she said. "Was Ruth your sister?"

"Yes."

"How old was she when she died?"

"Fifteen." The lump in my throat got bigger.

"And how old were you?"

"Seventeen."

Then she said something to me that no one else ever had since Ruth died: "That must have been very difficult for you."

"Yes, it was," I said. I felt tears well up and fought hard to keep from crying.

Her remark eased some of the tension I was feeling as we approached Smith Lodge, a small dark-brown wooden building on the edge of the grass just across a dirt road from one of the playing fields. As we approached, we could hear the bubbling of a nearby creek and kids' laughter. To my right, I saw several boys and girls gingerly putting their feet in the icy water and laughing as they quickly pulled them out.

We walked to the back of the lodge to enter the center. There was a small screened in porch, and on the outside frame a plaque that read *Ruth Gottscho Dialysis Center*. I swallowed hard again.

One of the nurses held open the screen door for us. "Hello," she said easily. "Come on in."

We entered a cramped but cheerful room with two metal desks and chairs on one side for medical staff, and three recliners, each next to a dialysis machine, on the other. Two of the recliners were occupied by kidney campers receiving dialysis treatments. Each had tubes leading from a vein in the arm to the machine.

One was a twelve-year-old boy watching a small TV next to him. He was very thin and had dark skin and a generous amount of black hair. When we entered, he gave us a big smile. We stopped by his chair and asked him what was happening. He was very articulate.

"My blood goes through this tube from my body through a filter in the machine. It cleans the blood and sends it back through the other tube."

"Does it hurt?" Bob asked.

"No. Mostly it's boring."

A sweet-looking girl with big round glasses was sitting in another recliner. She looked about ten. When we talked to her, we found out she was thirteen. The nurses later told us kids with kidney disorders often have growth problems; some take growth hormones to try to close the gap.

A nurse was leaning over a small table, writing in a looseleaf notebook. Sitting at the table was a girl with chronic kidney disease who didn't yet need dialysis. She had stopped in to take her medications.

We could feel the camaraderie between the staff and the kids. After the nurse returned the notebook to the desk, she began setting up a karaoke machine so the girl getting dialysis could sing her favorite songs while undergoing treatment. I found myself warming up to the kids and staff, though I had expected to remain aloof.

Tamara, the lively energetic pediatric nephrology nurse in charge of the unit, had come from Arizona and brought a couple of kidney campers with her. She was very warm and welcoming.

"It's wonderful," she said, "what your mother and the foundation did to make sleep-away camp possible for kids on dialysis."

"I agree," I said, and, at that moment, I meant it.

Despite the feelings of resentment and jealousy I felt toward Mom, she had done a lot to improve the lives of kidney kids. But I remained very uncomfortable in the unit, and my spirits lifted considerably after we returned to the pickup spot for campers.

Karen was waiting for us, and she gave us each a big hug. "Can't wait to go home," she said.

CHAPTER 26

THE GROUP HAD STIRRED UP MY EMOTIONS, and long re-pressed feelings of anger sometimes bubbled up outside it. I tried to control them, but often enough I couldn't.

We had a family picnic in our backyard two days after Karen came home from camp. There were twelve of us altogether: Bob, me, Karen and Daniel, Mom, Aunt Reba and Uncle Alfred, and five adult cousins.

It was late afternoon that sultry August. Happily, the towering oak tree on the western edge of our backyard provided ample shade.

We were seated around two narrow six-foot aluminum tables placed together end to end. I had covered them with cotton table-cloths—one a dark green with small flowers, the other a deep or-ange with a pattern of little leaves outlined in red and green. We sat on comfortable dark green plastic chairs from Home Depot. On each of the tables, a small painted wooden basket contained a flow-ering plant.

We were eating hot dogs and burgers that Bob had grilled a few feet away near the back of the house. He'd made his mother's recipes for cole slaw (cabbage, julienne carrot slivers, thin onion slices, chopped parsley, oil, and vinegar), and potato salad (chunks of small red potatoes, onion, parsley, a touch of oil and vinegar, and mayonnaise, garnished with slices of hard boiled eggs). Cut up ripe red Jersey tomatoes completed the main course.

To keep the mosquitoes and wasps at bay, we had put two plates of food scraps on the grass a number of feet away. They seemed to be working.

"So how was camp?" Uncle Alfred asked Karen.

"Okay," she answered without enthusiasm.

I sat there, and my stomach tightened.

"What did you do there?" Aunt Reba ventured.

"We had to go swimming every morning, and the water was freezing. I didn't want to go in, but my counselor made me."

"Did you sing around the campfire?" asked my mother, recalling one of her favorite activities when she was a camper.

"Yeah, but it was at night, and it was cold," said Karen.

"Did you have any kidney campers in your cabin?" my mother continued, and I felt a lump building in my throat.

"I don't know."

"You probably did and didn't know it," my mother said. "That's what's so wonderful about the program. The kidney campers sleep in bunks with regular campers and do all activities with them."

I felt my face get red, and a deep anger began to rise inside me. I tried to change the subject. "Would anyone like another hot dog or burger?"

"No, thanks," said several at the table.

"How's the camp program going?" asked one of my mother's cousins.

"It's going great," said Mom. "We visited camp in July to meet some of the kidney campers, and they're terrific kids. They came from all over the country. We spent a lot of time in the dialysis center, where the kids needing treatments go three times a week."

By then, Karen and Daniel had left the table to climb on the swing set behind our detached garage. The adults remained at the table.

I couldn't stand listening to the conversation, and I sat there with a stone face.

Up till then, Bob had been busy eating. He had worked the grill until he could sit down after some of us had already finished.

He joined the conversation. "The dialysis center is really amazing," he said. "We were given a tour on Friday when we picked up Karen. How many kidney kids are up there?" he asked my mother.

"I'm so *sick* and *tired* of *hearing* about it!" I cried out as I jumped up. My voice came from somewhere deep inside me. "I don't want to hear any more."

I threw my napkin on the table, pushed my chair back, and stormed up the steps to the side door. I jerked it open, marched through the kitchen, and settled onto the rocker in the living room. I was crying and heaving silently. For a few moments, it was hard for me to catch my breath.

I sat in that rocking chair in the darkened room—the sun was low by then and no one had turned on the light. I had expected Bob to follow me, but he hadn't. I was alone for what seemed like forever. I cried softly and rocked slowly back and forth.

Finally, my mother came into the living room and sat down on the wing chair opposite me. In her early seventies and gray, she was still very pretty, despite her pained look. She twisted a handkerchief in her hands and became teary.

". . . I'm sorry, Mom, but I don't want to hear about her any more. It's always Ruth, Ruth, Ruth."

"We tried our best, but I guess we failed you." Her voice broke. "At the time we didn't know any better. We had a sick child. . . ." She looked down and continued to finger the damp cloth.

That was a big admission I hadn't heard before. But then she went on, "What you fail to realize is how hard it was having a sick child. You have two healthy children. You have to understand what I went through. You never think about my feelings and how hard it was for me." Then the direction of her conversation shifted, and I was caught by surprise.

She got weepy. "As hard as it was to lose Ruth, it was ten times harder to lose your father. When Ruth died, we had each other. Now I have nobody, and I'm so lonely . . ." She blew her nose.

Although I felt she was being a little manipulative, I also felt sorry for her, and it flashed into my mind that she might be jealous of me: My kids were healthy, and I had my husband, whom she adored.

Just then one of my mother's cousins entered the living room. "Is everything all right?" she asked.

We're fine," my mother said. "We'll be out in a minute."

She turned and left.

I heard Bob's footsteps in the kitchen and then running water. People were helping to clear the table. Plastic dishes were going into a large bag for recycling, and platters and bowls being deposited on the counter. I knew he and I would talk about it later.

I pulled myself together and got up. "I'm going to run upstairs and wash my face," I told Mom. "I'll be back down shortly. Why don't you join the others outside, and we'll have dessert."

We gave each other a half-hearted hug, and I pecked her on the cheek. I wanted to close the gap between us but still needed to work through my anger. She wanted me to understand things from her point of view. That was fine, but she still didn't seem to be considering my feelings. Eventually, I would have to accept the fact that she wasn't going to change. It was going to require more work for me to get there.

AFTER EVERYONE LEFT, I TOLD BOB, "When you began asking Mom about the kidney camp program, I felt really angry and betrayed. You know what an open wound that is for me, but you pushed on anyway. I felt like you had deserted me."

We were sitting on opposite ends of the couch in the living room. The light behind him cast him in silhouette, though I could still see his serious demeanor.

" . . .I can't censor everything I say to make sure it won't hurt you," he said after a long pause. "It doesn't mean I don't understand your feelings. I'm not you, and I have a right to ask questions if I'm curious about the camp program without thinking first, *Will what I say hurt Judy?*"

I looked at his face, wearing such an earnest expression of love and concern, and I got it. I had put him in an untenable position. "I guess I'm being really unfair. It's just that I felt like such a caged animal with nowhere to turn. You're certainly on my side, and I can't expect you to feel what I feel."

We hugged, and I felt better. "I just wish my mother could understand that acknowledging my loss doesn't diminish her loss. It's not a competition."

CHAPTER 27

I ATTENDED WEEKLY GROUP THERAPY MEETINGS in Harriet's office for several years. During that time, two members of our original group left, and several new people joined us on Wednesday evenings.

After a year in group, Sandy met the man of her dreams. "We're so compatible!" she exclaimed. "We've never had an argument, and we never will!" They got engaged, and she left the group. Two years later, she sent us a photo of their twin girls.

Sunny left without any explanation after just a few weeks.

Andrew was the first man in the group. He was a tall, handsome, gangly guy, with a winsome grin. He was married, had two young daughters, and his wife was expecting. They had serious communication problems. He was self-effacing and likable. I had been concerned about being able to talk honestly once we became coed, but I liked and trusted Andrew.

Gina, Sue Ann, and I, the three remaining members of the original group, continued for a number of years. Other men and women joined us. Some dropped out after several sessions; others stayed for years.

After our group had convened in Cresskill for a couple of years, Harriet gave up her office there. By then, she had expanded the back of her home in Fair Lawn to include a large room off the kitchen that accommodated our group. We entered through a sliding door off a patio. It contained a large oval table that seated up to ten people. There was enough room for Harriet to open it for holiday functions with her family.

John Burn, the therapist who had assisted her with the group in Cresskill, did not continue once we moved. His confirmation in one of our early group sessions that I had a right to my feelings, particularly the anger associated with my sister's death, was very helpful.

Group therapy was very good for me. Aside from being in a place to deal with the loss of my sibling, I learned how to be more assertive. Once, shortly before one Mother's Day, I was talking about how much I dreaded the holiday as it approached, even after I had my own children. "My mother was always sad on that day, and I felt the burden of having to make her happy," I told the group. "I hated having to pick out a suitable card for her. It had to be funny with no terms of endearment. The actual day always revolved around her, and it was depressing."

I was about to go on when Harriet noticed another group member looking sullen. "What's going on?" she asked. The woman started talking about her feelings about Mother's Day. I refused to remain silent.

"It was hard for me to bring the subject up, and I'd like to finish what I was saying," I interjected. Harriet and the other group members turned their attention back to me.

"I asked my mother if she gets sad on Mother's Day because of Ruth, and she said, 'Yes.' Her response liberated me. I realized my angry feelings on that day didn't come out of left field."

"When your mother sees you, she also sees the child who isn't there," Harriet explained. It was a revelation—one of those *aha* moments. I experienced it only because I had expressed my need to finish what I was talking about.

At that point, I said I wanted to give the other person a chance to speak. I was learning how to assert myself but didn't want to be the focus of attention for too long. It took a while for me to be spontaneous and not worry that asserting myself might cause another person to be angry with me. Group was a safe place to learn how to do this.

I worried about my kids much more than other parents did, and I was able to talk about that in group, too. I knew first-hand that a child can die and, as a result, tended to be overprotective of Karen and Daniel. I learned in group that I didn't have complete control over them and needed to let them be kids if they were going to thrive as grown-ups.

When I brought up my feelings of dread, Mitch, a newer member of group and a father of a young daughter, said, "I worry about my child too, but I don't think she's going to die every time she steps outside." His comment was sobering, and I remembered it often as the kids were growing up. I wasn't able to get my worry level down to that of other parents, but being aware of it and knowing where it came from helped me keep it under wraps for the most part.

Laura was in the group for a few years. I liked her. We seemed to be on the same page in many ways, and I empathized with her.

She had a pretty face but was very overweight. She had been unsuccessful sustaining a meaningful relationship with a man, perennially attracting ones with emotional problems. As a result, her relationships were short-term and unsatisfying.

In one session, she told the group she was furious with me over a remark I'd made the previous week about her latest failed relationship. Because it seemed a pattern, I'd suggested she check with the group at the beginning of a relationship. Laura looked at me with rage in her eyes.

"When I talked about the problems I had with this guy, you said I should've discussed my feelings with the group before deciding to date him," she said coldly. "Your suggestion that I consult the group before making a move was insulting."

I felt as if she'd punched me in the gut, and a shiver went through my body. Anger directed at me was difficult to handle. I cringed and felt numb.

Harriet tried to assuage the situation. "Laura, I'm sure Judy said that out of her caring and concern for you."

That's true, I thought.

She didn't answer. Instead, she grabbed her jacket and pocketbook and stormed out, and she never returned.

Harriet had a policy of not talking about group members when they weren't there, so we never discussed my confrontation with Laura.

After several years, Harriet also stopped smoking. She was diagnosed with heart disease and had by-pass surgery. "Quitting was the hardest thing I've ever done," she told us, "but I had no choice." She chewed nicotine gum for a while, and then sucked on Life Savers.

CHAPTER 28

Being in the group helped me realize that having a sister who had died when we were growing up was significant and had had a huge impact on me, and that it was okay to have conflicting feelings about the loss. "What you feel is what you feel," we all kept saying. What you did with these feelings was what mattered.

I accepted this intellectually, but I was not yet able to emotionally.

In addition to what I learned there, I had a hunger to see whether articles or studies had been written on the effect a child's serious illness and death had on siblings.

That was early April 1987. Karen and Daniel were in elementary school, and I was working part time. I decided to do some research at the Fairleigh Dickinson University library in Teaneck. It was part of the Bergen County Cooperative Library System, which enables a patron of any town library in the county to use any other in the system.

The campus was a five-minute car ride from home. As I drove there, my heart was beating a mile a minute. Though it was a cool Spring day, I was sweating. I knew it would be emotional, and I was apprehensive.

I parked the car in the lot and found the campus map at the beginning of the path that ran along the Hackensack River—the border of the Teaneck part of the campus. A walking bridge over the river led to the school buildings on the Hackensack side.

As I gazed at the map, I heard a voice behind me. "What're you looking for?"

I turned around. A campus security guard was sitting in his car. He was middle aged, with thinning gray hair. He gazed at me through metal-framed sunglasses and smiled.

"The library."

"Halfway down the path, take the stairs on the left, and when you get to the top it'll be right in front of you."

"Thanks."

It was a chilly day, but the sun was shining on the river, making it sparkle. I noticed the water level was up. *Must be high tide,* I thought. I looked for ducks or other wildlife but saw none. Still it was very pretty, and I made a mental note to take a walk along the river soon with Bob.

Despite being the more metropolitan of the two FDU campuses—the other one was in tony Madison—there were beautiful trees lining the path along the river that were starting to bud. As I strode along, my nerves settled. I climbed the stairs and headed for the building. The setting was serene.

Sure enough, there it was. *Weiner Library*, read a white stone slab to the right of the main doors. Next to the name was a huge bronze relief of three lean figures—two standing men and a seated woman.

Passing through the library doors, I felt an immediate sense of purpose. *This is a university library where students conduct serious research,* I thought, *and I am joining them to pursue my own.* I felt both excited and anxious.

I made my way upstairs to the reference room. It was huge, with rows of fluorescent lights shining down from the high ceiling, and heavy dark wooden tables with high-backed slatted chairs taking up most of the floor space. Tall casement windows, spaced evenly along the walls, had wide blinds raised halfway. I could see the river through the bottom half of the windows that faced west, between them metal shelves filled with books.

I wasn't sure how or where to begin. I found the reference librarian, a woman just past middle age with short black hair and a clear complexion. She smiled at me, and I took a deep breath. "I'm looking for articles, or studies, that have been done on the effect of serious childhood illness and death on healthy siblings."

"Print journals are downstairs," she said. "Your best bet is to check the indexes for *Psychological Abstracts.*"

"Thanks."

I made my way down the stairs and entered a room equally as large and dominated by the same heavy tables. In addition, tall carrels sat in the center of the room. The periodicals librarian—a young, attractive blonde—was perched on a low-back stool behind a faux walnut desk. It was waist high in the middle, where she was sitting, and as tall as I was on either side, large, austere, and modern.

"Where are the *Psychological Abstract* indexes?" I asked.

"On the metal shelves around the corner," she said, pointing to the right.

I sat down at the long wooden table closest to the shelves that housed the volumes I needed. Each one was thick and heavy. As I began searching through them, I again felt a keen sense of purpose.

I spent several hours going through the indices and a few articles of interest. I jotted down the ones I wanted. It was getting late; I'd have to make a second trip to get copies of what I wanted to read.

A FEW DAYS LATER, I RETURNED and filled out half a dozen yellow call slips with the information the librarian needed to pull the articles I wanted. She handed them to a younger woman, probably a college student, standing beside her, who left. "Patrons can't go downstairs to retrieve the actual periodicals," she explained. "That's done by someone on staff. She'll find them and bring them up for you."

It didn't take long. The red-headed assistant handed me the periodicals, and I brought them to the table. I felt lightheaded, and handled the magazines as if they were made of precious stuff. I began to read.

Literature on sibling illness and loss was sparse, but what there was validated my own feelings. I was particularly interested in reading about the effects on siblings of a child dying following a prolonged catastrophic illness. Several mentioned anger toward a sick sibling that the healthy child often feels but buries deep inside, expressed in wishing the child were dead so things would get back to normal. The well child can also feel jealous of the sick one getting so much of their parents' attention.

As soon as that death wish comes true, the surviving child often feels a terrible guilt. When Ruth was sick, I'd been deeply fearful she was going to die. Yet sometimes I must have wished she were dead, which led to feelings of anger and guilt. Studies showed that, when a healthy child wishes that her seriously ill sibling would die, he or she is more likely thinking, "Are you *really* going to *die?*"

Maybe that's why I'd sucked my thumb much longer than most other kids. I had sought comfort in the storm. I'd stopped after I woke up at a slumber party when I was about twelve and heard other girls talking about me. "Can you believe Judy still sucks her thumb?" one of them whispered.

I also read that the healthy sibling can feel responsible for the chronically ill sibling's death—especially if the healthy child ever threw something at the sick one and was admonished for it. I remember throwing the hairbrush at Ruth and my mother screaming at me.

According to some research, surviving siblings sometimes seem indifferent or uncaring after their brother or sister dies. Adults may think these kids are heartless and cruel. Surviving siblings may act silly, fool around, or laugh uproariously. Kids express their grief in many ways, but it doesn't mean they're not hurting inside.

It validated my feelings to read articles that talked about the anger a surviving sibling can also feel over the enshrinement of a dead brother or sister. When my parents established the foundation in memory of Ruth, I recalled again how angry I had felt, and then how guilty about being angry. *For God's sake,* I'd wanted to shout, *can't you pay attention to me now? Why is everything always about Ruth?*

The surviving sibling often feels very lonely. That's because she usually loses her parents emotionally as well as her brother or sister.

(My mom and dad formed a tight bond of mutual sorrow, and I felt I was outside it.) If another relative or family friend doesn't reach out to the child, she suffers greatly, and working through the loss is much more difficult.

The feelings I brought up in group were again validated when I read about some of the things my parents did after Ruth died. It wasn't just me. For example, parents sometimes compare their surviving child's display of emotion (or lack of emotion) with their own reactions. I remembered standing at my sister's grave with my parents and feeling numb. I could feel their unspoken criticism that I didn't seem as upset as they were.

A child's grief can be expressed in profoundly different ways, I read. I remembered how I'd cried only when I was alone; I'd felt I had to be strong for my parents and be there for them. Sometimes children don't know how to behave around their grieving parents, according to the literature. *Maybe that was the case with me.* I knew for sure that I'd repressed my feelings, not recognizing how angry I was at my parents and at Ruth.

My mother's grief predominated. How interesting that I didn't include my *father* when I thought this. With this revelation, I experienced a jolt of understanding: My father had also repressed his feelings about Ruth's death, and I hadn't recognized how much he was hurting.

I remembered my mother saying to me, "You have to take care of yourself. If anything happened to you, I couldn't bear it." It's a heavy burden that some grieving parents put on the surviving siblings when they make this kind of statement. What she'd said was not uncommon.

As I pored over the articles I had found, I felt a new sense of relief. *I'm not alone,* I thought. *What I'm feeling is okay.* "I'm normal," I laughed out loud and glanced at people sitting at nearby tables, who showed no sign of having heard me.

Negative self-image. . .worries about your own health. . .high anxiety. . .keeping thoughts and feelings to yourself. I wasn't the only bereaved sibling who had reacted in these ways!

Listen up, everyone! I wanted to shout. *I'm okay—just a little crazy, and mixed up for more than twenty years because my sister was sick her whole life and died when she was fifteen.*

It hurt, but things were getting better.

I made copies of the articles I had found and put them in a folder labeled *Research on Sibling Loss.* It was another step in recognizing and coming to terms with the enormity of my loss.

CHAPTER 29

THE RANGE OF FEELINGS I'D HAD since Ruth died were validated by professionals who had studied sibling loss. Anger, pain, loneliness, and numbness are not unusual when a brother or sister dies. It's like experiencing a lot of discomfort after a medical procedure and the surgeon assuring you that your reaction is normal.

But soon I realized that squirreling myself away in a library, reading articles about the effects of sibling loss, wasn't enough. I also had an overwhelming desire to meet others who had lost a sibling when they were growing up.

But how to find them?

I had set up an office in the smallest room on the second floor of the house. It measured eight by ten feet with a built-in blond wooden desk, a tan fabric-covered metal desk chair, and a multicolored area rug. Double-hung windows faced west and north, providing lots of light in the afternoon and cross ventilation. I still needed a reading chair and lamp.

A desktop computer sat in the middle of the desk; to the left, a phone. I began searching for national organizations for bereaved siblings. I was a novice when it came to the computer, but I punched in "sibling loss." To my amazement, *Rothman-Cole Center for Sibling Loss* popped up. It was based in Chicago, and Jerry Rothman was a bereaved sibling! He had a doctorate, was a therapist, and had founded the organization.

I nervously wrote down the phone number and thought through what I wanted to say.

"Hello, is Dr. Rothman there. . . ?"

"Hello, I'd like to get more information about your organization. . . ."

"Hello, I'm a bereaved sibling and I want to find other people like myself. . . ."

Th*ey were all good opening lines,* I thought. *All I have to do is make the call!*

Finally, I picked up the phone and dialed the number.

"Hello," said a woman with a pleasant voice, "how can I help you?

"My sister died when we were growing up," I said, "and I wanted to know more about your organization. May I talk to Dr. Rothman?"

"I'm sorry, he's with a patient right now, but I'll be glad to help you."

"My sister died over twenty-five years ago, and I'm just beginning to deal with the loss," I told her. "I'd like to meet other people who've had a similar experience. Is there any group like yours in the New York area?"

"I don't know of any other organizations like ours, but in two weeks The Compassionate Friends is holding a weekend retreat for bereaved siblings in Kansas City, Missouri. As a matter of fact, Dr. Rothman is going to lead a couple of workshops there."

My head began to buzz. Had I heard her correctly? A weekend conference devoted to sibling loss?

She told me whom to speak to and suggested I make sure to sign up for Jerry's workshops. "He's very good," she said.

The Compassionate Friends. I knew about the group and loathed it. I didn't want to have anything to do with bereaved parents. Every time I read or heard about it, I seethed inside. My parents were more than enough to handle. I didn't need to get involved with a whole organization devoted to people who had lost children. But a weekend that centered around sibling loss—that was different story.

I called the organization's headquarters, and the person I talked to directed me to their affiliate for the Kansas City Region (MO-KAN), which was co-sponsoring the weekend with The Family Study Center at the University of Missouri-Kansas City. It was a working seminar called *When Brothers and Sisters Die: Gathering Ways to Help.*

My excitement was palpable as I dialed the number. I told the person who answered the phone about my interest in participating in the workshop.

"There's still room if you want to attend," she said. "Once we receive your registration fee, we'll send you detailed information about the seminar." She gave me the phone number for the hotel where the event was going to be held. "If you call right away, you'll be able to take advantage of the special conference rate."

The days passed quickly, and before I knew it I was heading for the airport. I still hated to fly, but it seemed as if the four-day week-end had been meant for me. As I was winging westward, I thought, *Serendipity has brought me here, and I'm going to make the most of it.*

I GOT TO THE HOTEL LATE THURSDAY AFTERNOON. The lobby was huge, with wall-to-wall black-and-gold carpeting, faux gold chandeliers, and music in the background.

I checked in and rode up the elevator to my room on the fourth floor, decorated in brown and green with two double beds, an upholstered chair, and a wooden desk. I was happy the window was one I could open to let in fresh air. I've never felt comfortable in hotel rooms with sealed windows that depend on blowing in dry air for heating and cooling.

Once I was there, I got very nervous. I didn't know a soul and wondered whether there would be attendees in their forties or I'd be considerably older than the others. I washed my face, put on fresh lipstick, ran my fingers through my short hair (I never use a comb), and went down to the lobby coffee shop to get something to eat. I treated myself to one of my favorite sandwiches—tuna salad on toasted wheat with lettuce and tomato. It was accompanied by a dill pickle and a side of cole slaw. By the time I'd finished eating, a registration table had been set up in the lobby.

When I ambled over, the two women and one man behind it were very friendly. They smiled. "Where are you from?" one of the women asked in a Midwestern accent.

"New Jersey."

"Oh, I think you've come the farthest of *anybody*," she said.

"Will I be the oldest?"

"Oh, my *goodness*, no," she replied. "We have all ages attending, even older than yourself." I felt a surge of relief.

She handed me the weekend schedule and directed me to the ballroom, where the opening reception was getting underway. "We'll see you again, I'm sure," she said, and turned her attention to the next person in line.

I entered a large meeting room full of lots of subdued chatter. I picked up a soft drink from the bar area and stood back, surveying the crowd. There were younger people, but others looked to be more my age.

I smiled at one younger woman standing with three others; she smiled back and motioned for me to join them. We introduced ourselves, and I found out they were members of a sibling support group connected with The Compassionate Friends chapter co-sponsoring the weekend.

The woman who had motioned to me asked, "Are you here alone?" She had a friendly demeanor and raised her hand to brush the shoulder length blond hair off her face.

"Yes. I found out about the conference from the Rothman-Cole Center in Chicago. My sister died more than twenty-five years ago, when we were teenagers, and I haven't yet processed the loss."

"Well, you've come to the right place," said one of the other women—a pert brunette in her forties. She had lost a brother in a car crash two decades before. "I'm still feeling sad and trying to come to terms with it."

The others had also lost siblings when they were younger—one had a brother who'd died before she was born. "It still affects me," she said.

The accounts of these losses sent shivers down my spine, and my eyes began to tear. I felt very grateful that I had found out about the weekend. It was going to be good.

We talked a bit more, then broke to go over to the *hors d'oeuvres* table. I filled a plate with some crackers, cheese, and grapes, and stepped back again. I looked around and saw a distinguished-looking gentleman not much older than me standing alone, nursing a cocktail. He had a full head of graying hair, a black mustache, a closely cropped salt-and-pepper beard, and large, black-rimmed glasses. He sipped his drink as he eyed the crowd. I wandered over.

"Hi, I'm Judy Eichinger. I assume you're also here for the sibling loss seminar."

"I'm Jerry Rothman," he said as he shook my hand.

I felt light-headed. "Jerry Rothman!" I exclaimed a bit too loudly. "I found out about this weekend from your office!" I told him about my search.

"I'm glad my staff is doing its job," he said with a twinkle in his eye. I was charmed by him and his Chicago accent.

"I'm very happy to meet you. Which workshop will you be leading?"

"I'm doing a couple. One's about the guilt many young people feel after the death of their sibling."

"Wow. That alone is worth the price of admission." I blushed, feeling my remark was a bit silly, but he didn't seem to mind.

"I'm also leading a discussion called 'The Uniqueness of Grieving for Kids.'"

"That sounds good, too. I know you lost a sibling growing up," I added. "What happened? How old were you?"

"When I was eleven, my eighteen-year-old brother died from an accidental gunshot wound while he was practicing target shooting. . . . And you?"

"My sister was born with almost no kidney function and died when she was fifteen and I was seventeen. I'm still trying to come to terms with the whole thing."

Jerry told me that he and his friend, Tom Cole, who'd also lost a brother in childhood, had established the Center for Sibling Loss two years before. It was located at the Southern School, a learning facility for emotionally disturbed children. Jerry was the school's executive director.

"A large percentage of our kids have lost a sibling," he said.

He eventually excused himself to take care of some personal business. We parted after agreeing to talk more during the weekend.

I approached several other people and introduced myself. All were warm and friendly and eager to share their stories. One woman around my age had suffered a double whammy: She had lost her sister growing up and a child from cancer. She was attending the weekend with her twenty-five-year-old daughter.

I felt giddy as the reception wound down. Who would have guessed a little more than two weeks before that I'd be in Kansas City attending a sibling-loss seminar? It seemed almost surreal. Workshops were beginning in the morning, and I headed to my room to review the schedule. I didn't want to miss a thing. I had already revamped my negative feelings about The Compassionate Friends. If a chapter of the organization was a co-sponsor of the weekend, it couldn't be all *that* bad.

CHAPTER 29

THE FIRST WORKSHOP WAS SCHEDULED for 9:30 a.m. I decided to attend Dr. Rothman's "Recognizing the Guilt." The Regents Room, where it was being held, was a windowless room containing five long, green-skirted tables, one behind the next, each seating eight. In front stood a podium and white board.

I chose a seat near the middle of the second table. All five had water pitchers and plastic cups laid out so at least one pitcher and set of cups were within reach of each participant.

When Dr. Rothman appeared ten minutes later, all the seats were filled, and a number of people had opened extra folding chairs that were stacked in the back and set them up next to the wall. My heart was racing in anticipation.

A member of the MO-KAN Compassionate Friends chapter spoke about the speaker's credentials and introduced him. There was polite applause. Then Jerry came forward and stood in front of the podium.

"Good morning," he said. He smiled and scanned the audience.

His eyes had the same twinkle that had animated them at the reception. He introduced himself and mentioned the sibling grief center in Chicago he had founded. Then he held up a reprint of an article from a familiar publication. "*People* magazine recently did a piece about our center and the work we do. I think they did a good job. Be sure to take a copy on your way out."

He invited us to call him "Jerry" but adopted a more serious demeanor when he said, "The first point I want to make is this: If you feel guilt, don't deny it. The feeling that we could have prevented the death is normal, especially for a younger child. 'Surely there was something I could have done . . . . ' is common among bereaved siblings.

"However, there may be some fantasy elements to the guilt we feel," Jerry continued. "Sure we think we could have done something. But we need to look at what happened from different perspectives," Jerry continued. "We need to accept ourselves as a little bit flawed."

He spoke as if he had been there himself, *and indeed he had*, I thought, remembering our conversation. But he didn't mention his brother during his presentation.

He talked about kids thinking they cause everything—the magic of primitive cultures. "They think they can actually make things happen. They also think wishes are the same as actions."

He moved on to survivor's guilt, which he said is "very normal: 'Why did my brother or sister die and not me?'"

Up until that moment, I had been hanging onto his every word. My mind veered off as I applied survivor's guilt to my own situation. Since my sister had died after being sick her whole life, I had concluded that my parents would have preferred losing me instead of her because they were so involved with her many health crises, and I was independent out of necessity. *She needed them more than I did*, I concluded, startled by this sudden revelation.

Jerry mentioned mother's guilt next. "They expect themselves to be able to protect their brood. When a mother loses a child, there's a certain amount of guilt there, too—the feeling of not having been a *successful* mother. It's a biological instinct.

"And there's some truth to this," he continued, "yet the world is an imperfect place—a mother can't *always* protect her brood."

I got very angry when he began talking about mothers. *I thought we're here to talk about bereaved siblings, not bereaved parents.*

Almost immediately, this thought was superseded by a jolting revelation: *My mother must have suffered enormous guilt after giving birth to a damaged child. . . . Perhaps she continued to punish herself after Ruth died, and I received the brunt of that anger.*

Jerry said something else that hit home. "There are also *degrees* of guilt. If there was a lot of *conflict* before the death, there's *more* guilt."

The conflict in my home growing up was just under the radar, I thought, *but it was definitely there.*

There were questions from the audience after he spoke, but I was deep in my own thoughts, unlocking doors. What Jerry said gave me permission to accept my feelings. It was very liberating.

On the way out, I picked up a copy of the *People* magazine reprint. I wanted to read it as soon as possible.

I GRAVITATED TO A WORKSHOP CALLED "Writing as Therapy" because I'd put pen to paper a number of times in my life to better understand my thoughts and feelings during moments of crisis.

The meeting room also had long tables and chairs, and there was a lined pad of paper and pen in front of each seat.

Marie Butler introduced herself. She had written a book, *Bereaved Sibling*, in 1978. "Writing about grief and healing helps get the feelings out, not just the emotions. . . . You want to get the feelings out before the emotions build up."

Marie gave us four topics and asked us to write a paragraph about each one. This is what I wrote:

1. Today I feel. . . .

Better, calm, open. I think I'm getting a lot out of the conference. I hope it lasts. But I still want to cry a lot when I read, or hear, about problems of siblings coping with their loss. I get emotional easily. Someone said recently that people who feel like crying when they read a story in the newspaper or hear a song, etc., haven't gotten all their emotions out.

2. What I enjoy telling my friends about you. . . .

This is a tough one for me because I never talk about my sister to anyone. I hate hearing other people talk about her. I'm still very angry. Yet I know we had a great relationship most of the time. But because I felt so lost as a person while she was sick (all her life) and after she died I feel selfish now (and guilty about it).

3. One thing I never got to tell you. . . .

It's going to be hard, real hard without you—that I'll miss you.

4. If I could have one day back I would. . . .

Want to talk honestly about our feelings about sickness and death and dying and how she felt and how I felt. I'd want to talk about it openly with each other and with our parents. Living with pretending was really a barrier.

My responses flowed out of me without thinking. When I reread them, I was shocked by what I had written. My answers were so revealing and honest. I could hardly speak after the exercise. If I did, I'd burst into tears. The answer that got to me the most was #3. Losing Ruth had hurt so much, and I'd never expressed to myself how deeply it hurt until that moment. I had written only one sentence, but it packed a wallop once I saw it in black and white.

Several of us, walking out of the workshop, agreed it had been a powerful exercise. One dark-haired girl in her early twenties had tears in her eyes, and they welled up when she tried to talk. Another young woman put her arm around her.

"I feel the same way," I told her.

A BUFFET DINNER WAS SERVED THAT EVENING. I helped my self to two pieces of roast chicken, rice, green beans, and salad, and sat with the mother and daughter I had met at the opening reception.

"I think it's amazing that you can reach out to your daughter after losing a child," I said. "It must be so nice to have each other's support."

"I remember what it was like when my sister died," the mother said. "And, you know, reaching out to my daughter helps with my own pain."

We talked about lighter matters. "I've never been to New York," said the mother, who lived in Kansas City. "It must be nice to live so close. Do you get to see a lot of shows?"

"Believe it or not, I haven't seen a single Broadway show this year," I confessed. "I usually go to the theater when friends or family visit. I've also never been to the top of the Empire State Building." They found that hard to believe.

"We'd love to see the Christmas show at Radio City," the daughter said.

"When you come to New York, let me know, and I'll go with you," I offered. "I saw it when I was growing up, and I loved it. The Rockettes are amazing, and the art deco design of the place is something to see."

AFTER DINNER, I WENT TO MY ROOM, put my bag and sweater on the bed, and sat down on the chair to read the People magazine article. I wanted to know more about Jerry Rothman and how he had handled the loss of his brother.

The two-page spread about Jerry and the Rothman-Cole Center for Sibling Loss was in a Q-and-A format. Early in the article, Jerry spoke movingly about his brother's death and how it had affected him. "When Joseph died, I was in sixth grade, and I had a terrible time in school. I got into trouble and did outrageous things to get attention, because from the time he died I felt pretty much neglected by my parents. Everyone idealized my brother and made me feel I had to follow in his footsteps, so I went to the opposite extreme."

He had felt he couldn't show his grief. "Part of it was the feeling that it would make my parents more upset if I was sad, so I replaced the sadness with acting out. I had a lot of fear and a lot of anger—anger at my brother for dying, anger at my parents for allowing it."

I empathized completely with what he was saying. Most of

what he felt was eerily similar to what I had experienced.

After talking about the lingering affects of it, Jerry answered questions about sibling loss in general. "After the death of a child, there is a tendency for parents to become overprotective and rein in the surviving kids. . . . This over-protectiveness can even interfere with the child's future relationships. . . . Children who have lost a sibling are less likely to marry whey they grow up, and if they do marry they are less likely to have children. They are so terrified by the pain of loss they suffered that they don't want to run the risk of it happening again." (I found out later that Jerry was married but didn't have children.)

As a psychotherapist who worked with troubled children, Jerry discovered that 25 percent of the kids he counseled had lived through the death of a brother or sister. " . . . I began to notice that the loss was an unrecognized cause of many of the problems they had."

Jerry and Tom Cole founded the Sibling Loss Center in 1985. It was the only organization in the country to focus solely on the issue of sibling bereavement.

I was very moved by what I had read and wanted to get to know more about the Center and the work they do. I hoped to get another chance to talk to Jerry before the end of the conference.

THE NEXT MORNING, I ATTENDED two more workshops. One was on the grief process, but it was mostly about things I'd already heard. The speaker described the differences between grief depression and general depression.

"Grief depression is the result of a specific loss," said the earnest, dark-haired young man with a master's degree in social work. "When someone has general depression they feel sad about everything."

He also identified the four stages of grief as numbness (shock), pining (hurt), dejection (void), and recovery. I couldn't relate to what he was saying.

The other workshop was about helping kids with their grief. The speaker was a genial middle-aged child psychologist with wisps of gray hair on the top of his head and more generous amounts of gray along the sides. He gave tips on how to provide immediate means of support to a child who has lost a sibling.

"Before you reach out to the child, ask yourself, 'What am *I* feeling?' Then you can put your feelings away and listen to the child.

"Know your expectations and why you're doing this," he continued. "Be a good observer. Watch for clues, and begin to feel with the child. Give the child permission to hurt and grieve. Let him know that whatever he's feeling is okay."

I especially liked what he said next: "Be guided by the child's needs, not yours. If you're not sure, call it *our* needs."

He concluded by saying, "Children and young adults will address their loss again and again, and each time they'll reach a new level of understanding."

THAT EVENING WAS A SIT-DOWN DINNER, and I got a chance to talk to Jerry again. We were both getting coffee at the end of the meal and settled at a nearby table.

"I got a lot out of your workshop on guilt," I said.

"I'm glad." He stirred his cup. "You know, our sibling grief center is planning an experiential weekend later this year or early next for people like you who have lost a brother or sister when they were growing up. Would you be interested in coming?"

"Absolutely," I replied without hesitation.

"We've also started a website for bereaved siblings. I'd like you to take a look at it and tell me what you think."

"Sure." He took a pen and pad from his inside jacket pocket, jotted down the web address, and handed it to me. I pulled a small ringed notebook from my pocketbook, wrote down my contact information, and gave it to him to add to his mailing list.

I told him how touched I had been by the *People* magazine article. He seemed pleased. As much as I wanted to know more about his relationship with his brother, I didn't feel it was the right time to ask.

Jerry told me his wife was also a therapist, and that they often led workshops together. They sometimes attended conferences in New York.

"Let me know when you're in town," I told him. "I'm only a half hour away from the west side of Manhattan."

THE NEXT DAY, BEFORE LEAVING, I checked out the book display in the lobby. There were a number of titles on sibling loss for kids and adults. I browsed through several, then zeroed in on one: *Losing Someone You Love, When a Brother or Sister Dies*, by Elizabeth Richter. I flipped through the thin, attractive volume. It spotlighted fifteen youngsters who had lost a brother or sister. Each short chapter featured a full-page black and white photo of the surviving sibling accompanied by a one- or two-page personal account in which they talked openly about their feelings. All but one death had occurred when they were teenagers.

My hands trembled as I leafed through the book. It was just seventy-eight pages long, but it was a treasure trove of sibling-loss experiences. I bought it and knew I would devour every word on the plane going home.

By the time I left the conference, I had the names and addresses of a number of people I had met. Two of them had started sibling-loss support groups through their local Compassionate Friends chapters. I was seeing the organization in a whole new light.

Several young people I had met were going to start a sibling-loss newsletter that would publish poems and short prose by bereaved siblings. Others vowed to keep in touch by mail. It was another step for many of us on a journey we'd never wanted to take. That weekend we discovered that meeting others on the same journey made our loss easier to bear.

CHAPTER 30

THE FOLLOWING MORNING, I took the hotel shuttle to the airport to catch my return flight. The sun shone brightly, and the forecast for Newark was clear. It seemed certain the weather wasn't going to delay my trip home.

Security went smoothly. I had a short walk to the gate. Judging from the number of people waiting to board, my flight was going to be far from full. *Maybe I'll luck out and won't have anyone sitting next to me,* I thought.

Once on board, I settled into my aisle seat over the wing. Other passengers sat down in front of and behind me, but no one took the center or window seats next to me.

I wasn't that terrified of the return flight. Perhaps it was the sunlight pouring through the window or my eagerness to read my new book. I dug it out of my carry-on tote before we pulled away from the gate.

Our plane took its place in the short takeoff queue, and soon we had moved to the head of the long runway. The pilot revved up the engines, and we began to roll. As we increased speed, I prayed to get there safely, as I always did. But I felt exhilarated when we lifted off the ground and banked to the right.

Once we reached cruising altitude, we seemed to glide weightless through the sky, and the engines became quieter. The sun was high, and there were just a few scattered clouds.

I picked up the book, *Losing Someone You Love: When a Brother or Sister Dies*. I fingered the photo on the cover of a teenage boy leaning against a tree in a rural setting. He was gazing solemnly at some faraway place. I flipped through the pages and found his story midway through the book.

I went back to the beginning and started reading. The first-person accounts of what it was like to lose a sibling were honest, direct, and heart-wrenching.

All but one had been teens when their brother or sister died (the other sib had been twenty-two). They spoke openly about their pain, jealousy, and guilt. I felt the same kinship I had felt at the sibling-loss gathering. "I've been there, too," I whispered.

Several had lost a sibling in an auto accident. For others, like me, it'd been an illness. One girl's sister had been murdered; another had had a brother who committed suicide. Many were sharing their feelings for the first time.

Some felt guilt. One girl said she knew, deep down, her mother wasn't sorry her sister had died instead of her, but sometimes she felt guilty for surviving. I recalled Jerry Rothman's workshop about guilt and how prevalent it is among survivors.

Some of the teens talked about their parents being overprotective. They understood it intellectually, but it still bothered them. Others feared another beloved family member would die. Marc, whose baby brother had died of SIDS, was afraid his mother would go away and never come home.

The weekend seminar, and the book, helped me realize how common the fear of losing another family member was among bereaved siblings. Too often, when Bob or one of our kids left the house, I was afraid something would happen to them. It was an eye opener to discover that others felt the same way.

One teenager said she had to be very careful because, if anything happened to her, it would kill her parents. I was reminded of my mother's initial visit to my first apartment in the City. Ruth had died four years before. "Take care of yourself," she had said when she was leaving. "If anything happened to you, I'd die."

I was halfway through the book when I noticed the stewardess standing next to me. "Would you like something to drink?" she asked.

"Tomato juice, please, without ice." I laid the book on the seat next to me.

She opened a can, poured the contents into a plastic glass, and handed it to me along with a small bag of chips. I thanked her and put the chips in my bag. I finished the juice in time to toss the glass into the trash bag she offered as she passed by a second time. I closed the tray, picked up the book, and returned to where I had left off.

I read about a teen who tried to get closer to her parents without success. She described how shut out she felt.

Wow, I certainly felt that way after Ruth died.

Other things resonated with me, too. One teen had a recurring dream that her dead sibling was alive, and would wake up to the harsh reality that she was dead. Another felt jealous, in college, when younger brothers and sisters visited.

Two brothers reminisced about their younger sister, who'd had aplastic anemia and had been in and out of hospitals the final three years of her life. She'd told her family she was going to die a week before it happened.

Tears welled up in my eyes when I read that. I was pretty sure Ruth knew she was going to die. I remembered again her friend Lorre telling me about the time he and Ruth walked to the pond in Taylor Park, when he had invited her to throw a stone into the pond and watch the ripples it made, and she'd said, "I don't think mine will reach the other side."

Lisa, whose sister had been murdered, was featured toward the end of the book. Everyone had told her to be strong for her parents. She'd kept her feelings to herself, working hard not to cry. She wished someone had asked her how *she* felt.

Lisa also talked about doing poorly in school after her sister died. She'd cut classes and started getting into drugs. I recalled Jerry Rothman saying in the *People* magazine piece that twenty to twenty-five percent of the troubled kids he'd counseled had lost a sibling.

Lisa said she'd had mixed feelings about being interviewed for the book but then concluded it might help someone. She hoped that a young person who finds it difficult to talk to a family member or friend would read the book and feel less alone.

WHEN I FINISHED READING the seventy-eight-page volume, I wanted to hug all the young people who had spoken so honestly about their feelings. Almost every entry had an accompanying photo. I looked at each one and silently thanked them for agreeing to tell their story.

I leaned back against the headrest and thought about the past three days. At the conference, I had met and talked with many others who had lost a sibling, and in the book sixteen young people had described their loss in very moving, intimate ways. If this book had been available when I was seventeen, when Ruth died, and I had heard of it, it would have had a huge impact on my life.

One thing for sure: I no longer felt alone. Attending the workshop and reading the book helped me feel a part of a community and validated many of my feelings.

I slipped the book back in my tote as the pilot announced the beginning of our descent. With the time change, the sun was low enough to give the few puffy clouds an orange glow. I sat back, relaxed, and enjoyed the wondrous display of color.

CHAPTER 31

WHEN BOB PICKED ME UP at the airport, I hopped in the car and told him how meaningful it had been for me. "It was amazing. I met so many bereaved siblings, younger *and* my age, and listened to fabulous speakers. Everything I heard validated my feelings."

"That's great," he said as we pulled away from the curb. "I'm glad it was such a positive experience."

My mother's reaction was much more subdued.

For the last few months, I'd been working part-time for my mother. She was the CEO of the machine manufacturing company that, under my father's leadership, had become recognized and respected throughout the packaging industry.

Dad had died in 1971, nine months after Bob and I were married. The company vice-president had taken over the helm but, within a year, succumbed to a virulent virus he had picked up in Mexico while on a business trip.

A few weeks after his death, my mother'd made a momentous

decision. "I will *not* let all the sweat and tears my husband put into this business go down the drain," she had declared. "*I'm* going to run it."

Despite being a homemaker since she and my father had married thirty-nine years before, she took over the reins. She didn't have an engineering degree, let alone a college education, but she was determined to make it work.

"I'm very familiar with the business," she'd said in defense of her decision. "I accompanied my husband to trade shows and business meetings, and he included me in all his business decisions."

She had taken an accounting course at the American Management Association in New York City and became active in the Packaging Machinery Manufacturers Institute. She'd reached out to members of the organization she already knew through my father, as well as to many newer members. She had picked their brains, along with those of the management team already in place at the company.

Although she was short on engineering knowledge, she had innate public relations skills, and she used them to her best advantage. After losing my father—the love of her life— eleven years after her younger daughter died, she had decided she was going to become a businesswoman.

In the privacy of her home, my mom continued to be a very needy person who couldn't stand to be alone and was very hard on me if I didn't respond to her beck and call. But within the packaging community, she became a respected leader. For a number of years, the company remained at the top of its field, and Mom received well-deserved credit for keeping it there.

The factory/office building—which included a few private offices, drafting rooms, and cubicles for engineers, management, sales reps, and support staff—was on a long, quiet mixed residential/industrial block off busy Morris Avenue in Union, New Jersey. On one side were modest single-family homes on small, quarter-acre lots. The opposite side was lined with factory buildings fronted by narrow lawns, shrubbery, and a few trees. Most of the buildings were well maintained, although there were a couple of unkempt, empty properties—a harbinger of the future downturn in the industrial real estate market.

Several months after Daniel entered first grade, I'd wanted to go back to work part-time. My mother had been running the business for over ten years by then.

"Why don't you come work for me?" she had suggested. "You have public relations experience, and I need someone to oversee advertising and promotion."

"Okay," I'd said after thinking about it for a few days. It seemed like a win-win situation.

I went in on Mondays, Tuesdays, and Thursdays, though I was able to change the schedule when necessary.

Because I had traveled to the conference the previous Thursday, I had been out of the office for six days.

Most of my trip south from Teaneck to Union was on the Garden State Parkway. Trucks weren't allowed, so it was less nerve-wracking than taking the Jersey Turnpike. But there were always those drivers who drove too fast and zipped from one lane to another without signaling. The commute took about forty minutes, depending on traffic.

As usual, I parked my black Sable station wagon in the lot to the right of the building and ambled through the side door that opened onto one end of the large, sprawling factory floor. The place was humming with activity. It was an enormous space where machinists in one area made small parts used to build larger, in-line marking and coding machines—many of which my father had developed and patented. I turned left past an enclosed area that housed the accounting department and through the door to the front offices.

It was a few minutes past nine, and most employees were already at their desks. "Hi, Dottie," I said to a plain but pleasant middle-aged woman who had been a clerk with the company forever.

"Good morning," she said cheerfully. "How was your weekend?"

"Fine, thank you." Dottie didn't know I'd gone to Kansas City.

I poked my head into my mother's secretary's small office, which led to my mother's larger one. "Hello, Dee, how are you?"

She was about ten years older than I, with tight brown curls framing her face and tortoise-shell glasses, attached to a cord, that most often rested on her chest.

Dee had the raspy voice of someone who had chain-smoked for too many years. She looked up from her desk and smiled. "Hi, Judy, I'm fine. Your mom will be here shortly. Her car's being repaired, so one of the employees went to pick her up."

My small office, adjacent to my mother's much larger one, had been used by a middle manager who was no longer with the company. The space was dominated by a wooden desk on which sat a clunky computer monitor above a CPU, a keyboard, a telephone, and in/out boxes. The adjustable office chair behind the desk had seen better days, and a polished wooden chair sat on one side for visitors. The walls, painted a light green, looked faded and seemed to cry out for a fresh coat.

An oil painting of a serene Scottish meadow hung on the wall; it had been in my parents' house for many years, and Mom had moved it to the office shortly after she took over.

I settled behind my desk and checked my calendar. It would be a good idea to get something done before she arrived. Often she wanted to see me soon after she got there.

I was having serious doubts about continuing with the company; working for a relative, particularly if it's your mother, was not a great idea. I knew it was a tremendous opportunity, but I'd recently expressed my concerns to Bob. "If I want to maintain a good relationship with her, I may have to leave."

"Why? What's going on?"

"It's hard to keep things on a professional level. She often comes into my office and waylays me about a personal issue— maybe she didn't sleep all night, or she wants to fire her current housekeeper. I feel trapped."

"Can you tell her you're in the middle of something, that you'll talk to her when you're finished?"

"Thing is, I don't want to mix the personal with the professional when I'm there. She wouldn't do that with anyone else."

Actually, that wasn't quite true. I know Mom liked to vent to Dee. But when I was there, I was her first choice.

"The other thing is that sales are slowing down, and the first place Mom wants to cut is the advertising and marketing budget." I knew he'd be sympathetic. His graphic design firm had clients that made similar decisions. Companies often feel these expenses are the most expendable when they need to cut costs. "I think it'd be a terrible mistake," I concluded.

"I don't know how you can stop her from talking about personal issues. . . . But have you told her how important you feel marketing is to the health of the company?"

"We have a proposal on the table from an independent ad firm that I think is good and very reasonable. She seemed to agree with everything he said during his presentation, but now she's balking. 'We can't afford it,' she said after he left."

"It's not just your mother. It's corporate think. Sometimes they realize their mistake and come back to us with their tail between their legs."

I reached for the phone on my desk and made some calls. A half hour later, Mom came in, said hello to everyone, and, as she passed by, motioned to me to follow her.

It had been fifteen years since my father died, and the office of the president retained the same furniture. Mom's desk was the one Dad had used—polished walnut with a heavy glass slab on the top. It was large but not ostentatious. A high backed, dark brown leather chair sat behind it. A credenza the length of the desk sat on the floor behind her, and two upholstered chairs faced the desk on the other side. To the right, several feet beyond the desk, a sitting area contained a round, marble-topped table, a curved sofa, and two more upholstered chairs. When Mom took over, she'd had the chairs and sofa reupholstered. The couch was done in a solid, deep orange—her favorite color—and the chairs were covered with a pattern in which orange predominated. She had replaced the old beige carpet with one similar in color but with a nubbier texture. The walls were paneled in wood.

The room was very light, thanks to several large windows behind the sitting area. There was also a window behind the desk. All had cream colored drapes pulled to the side and wooden blinds to control the late afternoon sunlight and provide privacy when it was needed.

My favorite features were the small private bathroom that had a secret door paneled in the same faux wood as the wall, and an adjacent closet that contained a half-size refrigerator and paper supplies. "How's the car?" I asked her.

"It's okay——just needed an alignment."

Mom loved her white Lincoln Continental. She'd had it for a number of years, and the mileage was creeping up, though she used it mostly for local driving. If she traveled to see us or needed to go any distance, she had an arrangement with one of the men in the factory to drive her, and she paid him extra.

"I don't know if you remember," I'd said, "I went to Kansas City this past weekend to attend a bereaved sibling workshop."

"Yes. How was it?" She seemed preoccupied with something on the desk when she asked this.

"Great. I got a lot out of it."

"That's good."

Mom summoned her secretary to come in. I felt my eyes tear, and I turned away.

"I'll see you later," I said, and went back to my office.

WHEN I WAS AT THE COMPANY, I handled the occasional press release sent out about the business or the foundation. I remember one of them in particular. Mom had put together a rough draft of a story about how she had taken over the business after my father died. It included material about the foundation's beginnings. She had asked me to type it for inclusion in an upcoming packaging engineering periodical.

The draft she gave me read, "After Eva and Ira's daughter died of kidney failure, they began a foundation in her memory." It was well-written, but I added one word: "After Eva and Ira's *younger* daughter died. . . ."

The insertion of that one word had made a huge difference to me. In my mind, it established that I was also a presence, and I got a lot of satisfaction from making the change.

CHAPTER 32

B Y THE END OF THE SUMMER, I had made a decision: to stop working for Mom and look for a job with a non-profit organization. I knew it would pay less, but the work would be more meaningful.

I needed to tell her. I invited her to lunch at a neighborhood Italian restaurant that was one of her favorites.

"*Buon pomeriggio*," said the maitre d' as we entered the restaurant. "Good to see you," he said to Mom. "We have excellent fresh snapper today," he added, knowing it was one of her favorite dishes. She smiled, pleased by the attention.

He led us to a corner table, pulled out her chair, then mine. Once we were seated, he handed each of us a menu. "*Buon appetito,*" he murmured, bowed slightly and left to attend to a group of four men who had arrived just after us.

We both decided on the snapper special and gave the order to the waiter.

"What's the occasion?" my mother asked. She took a sip of

water. "Are you pregnant?"

I laughed. We both knew I had marked my forty-fifth birthday a couple of months earlier. But her query wasn't all tongue in cheek. She'd said long before that she'd hoped Bob and I would have four children, two for me and two for Ruth.

I took a deep breath before answering. "No, it's about work. I've enjoyed what I've been doing the last few months. It's been great, and I've learned a lot. But I want to change direction." I exhaled and took a sip of water before continuing. "I've done a great deal of thinking, and I'd like to get into the non-profit field. I'm also ready to work full- time, and I want to be closer to home."

Her eyes narrowed as she gazed at me. "What, I'm not paying you enough?"

"You're paying me more than enough, and I really appreciate it. I just want to go in a different direction." I decided not to bring up the other reason.

". . . I'm very disappointed," she declared, getting teary and looking away. "I was hoping you'd eventually take over the business."

"I know. But it's not what I want to do, and I need to find something nearer home, so I can be available to the kids when necessary." I reached for her hand. "If you want me to stick around until you find a replacement—"

"No, it's all right. We can't do much marketing now anyway because of the reduced sales. I'll ask one of the men to take over."

She told me again how disappointed she was, and I told her I was, too. Then the waiter arrived with our food. The snapper came over a bed of fresh spinach with garlic, and it was delicious. We ate in silence for a few minutes, and then I updated her on what the kids were doing. We finished and ordered decaf coffee.

My nose itched, a sign I was feeling guilty. But I knew I was doing the right thing for me.

The waiter brought a plate of biscotti along with the coffee. "On the house," he said.

"Thank you," my mother gushed. We consumed them in short order, along with the coffee. I paid the bill, and we left.

ONCE AGAIN, I WAS UNEMPLOYED. I spent the week at the desk in my small office upstairs, updating my resumé and looking through the daily paper. During the short time I worked for Mom, I'd gained valuable marketing experience. I made sure to list it as the first item under Work History.

I turned on the radio and set the dial to WQXR, the local classical music station. It kept me calm and focused.

Instead of going through the want ads, I searched the Business and Local News sections of the daily Northern New Jersey newspaper. There was an ad for a women's job fair the following Monday, sponsored by the Women's Rights Information Center, a non-profit organization in nearby Englewood. The organization helped women with housing, legal advice, and job information. The ad listed several of the schools, companies, and organizations that would be participating.

Some exhibitors were offering employment opportunities, others training. There were also going to be a resumé-writing clinic, a job-search support group, and a "dress-for-success" booth offering gently used professional clothing.

The fair would be held at a nearby women's club. The ad included a phone number for pre-registration. I called and gave them

my name, cut out the ad, and attached it to the draft of my new resumé.

THE FOLLOWING MONDAY, I wore a white blouse with a dark gray
pant suit, black pumps, and a black shoulder bag. I also brought a
portfolio of my work and several copies of my resumé. On a separate sheet I had listed three references.

The fair was scheduled to begin at nine-thirty. I left the house
at nine, drove to the venue fifteen minutes away, and turned into
the parking lot at nine-fifteen. To my amazement, it was almost
full. I pulled into the first vacant slot, turned off the engine, and
grabbed my purse and portfolio.

I was behind several other women. When we approached the
main building, we could see a long line extending from the entrance.
I took my place at the end, but soon an official-looking woman addressed those in line. "Have any of you pre-registered?" she asked.

"I have," I said, raising my hand.

"Follow me." She led me to a table with a much shorter line.
"There should be a name tag for you here."

Sure enough, when I reached the front of the line, a pleasant-
looking woman checked off my name and handed me a packet and
name tag. "Inside there's a list of exhibitors and a map showing
where to find them. Several women with WRIC name tags will be
circulating through the crowd to answer any questions."

I entered the building and sat down just inside the door. I
looked at the list of exhibitors. There were some companies offering entry-level jobs—banks, a couple of insurance companies, some
retail establishments. However, most were schools offering training
programs—computer schools, medical assistant or health aide

schools, even a couple of secretarial schools. I was disappointed.

I almost left but decided to stroll up and down the aisles before calling it quits. I sauntered past each table, looking at the exhibits and shook my head a couple of times when someone behind a table motioned me closer.

I was about to give up when I spotted a banner over a table toward the end of the last aisle: *The Career and Life Counseling Center*. I sidled over and began looking at the flyers and brochures. A pretty blond woman about my age, standing behind the table, smiled at me. I could see a hint of freckles on her nose and cheeks.

"Hi," she said in a warm, welcoming voice. "I'm Denise, and I'm the assistant director of the Center." She reached across the table and shook my hand.

"Nice to meet you." I introduced myself. "What does your organization do?"

"We offer job-search counseling, computer training, and non-traditional training courses for women."

"Oh?" I replied, intrigued. "What does that mean?"

"Training for women to go into the trades, such as carpentry, electrical work, and plumbing."

"I'm interested in getting a public relations job at a non-profit organization. Can you help me with that?"

"We have career counselors who meet individually with women to help them decide the best career path to take."

"Are you a county organization?"

"We're actually part of Bergen Tech, the county vocational technical school."

"I'd love to meet with you. Is that possible?"

"Absolutely." She handed me her card. "Give me a call tomorrow. We can set up an appointment to talk, and I'll also give you a tour."

I was excited. The place sounded wonderful, just what I was looking for.

"Great. I'll call tomorrow. Thanks so much."

I left feeling giddy. Something about Denise and the work they did intrigued me. I couldn't wait to talk further.

WHEN I CALLED THE NEXT DAY, she remembered me. "I'd love to sit down with you and tell you about my background and experience," I told her.

"How's Thursday at ten?"

"Great."

She gave me directions. The Center was in Hackensack, less than ten minutes from my house.

THURSDAY WAS VERY WARM. Although we were three weeks into September, it felt like a dog day in August. I slipped into a short-sleeved white cotton blouse, dark slacks, and a mint green, light-weight jacket. I brought my portfolio and copies of my resumé.

I wasn't sure exactly what outcome I wanted, just followed my gut.

I turned right off busy Hackensack Avenue, just past the north end of Bergen Tech, and followed a long, narrow driveway that dead-ended in the back. The one-story wooden building looked somewhat dilapidated. A weathered picnic table stood off to the side, and the structure itself needed a new coat of paint. I parked the car, got out, and was clobbered by the heat. At the front door, a sign invited me to ring the bell and enter.

Inside was a seating area with a large, worn dark rug on the floor, and a couch, some chairs, and a couple of small tables along the walls. Denise had told me to go through the door facing me and give my name to the receptionist.

I did and found an attractive woman in her thirties, with shoulder-length, honey-brown hair, behind the desk to my left. There was a slight gap between her two front teeth when she smiled, but that didn't detract from her good looks.

"Can I help you?" she asked in a deep, throaty smoker's voice with a slight Slavic accent.

"I have a ten o'clock appointment with Denise," I said, returning the smile.

"Have a seat. I'll call her." She pointed to a chair on the opposite wall.

There was another desk in the reception area with a woman about the same age as the receptionist sitting behind it, typing away on her keyboard, and, to the right, an open door. I could hear someone inside talking on the phone. Other female voices floated in over transoms from the back, creating a steady hum of vocal activity.

I had been seated only a few minutes when I saw Denise coming toward me. I stood up, we shook hands, and she told me to follow her.

She led me down a short hall and turned left. We passed one small, narrow office with the door ajar. I looked in and gave a start. "*Laraine!*" I exclaimed. She looked up.

"Judy! What're you *doing* here?"

Laraine lived in my neighborhood with her husband and two young sons. I saw them from time to time when they took walks past our house. We had originally met at a PTA meeting at the local elementary school. She was a social worker, and I knew she did career counseling. I had no idea she worked at the Center.

"I'm meeting Denise," I said.

"Stop by and see me before you leave."

Denise's office was next door. It was just as small and narrow but had a window. "That's why I picked it," Denise said.

She sat down behind the desk at the far end of the room and motioned for me to take the one opposite.

I gave her a copy of my resumé and described my previous work in private industry, including my last job doing marketing and PR for the family business.

She took a few minutes to read it.

"You have a lot of good experience."

"I'd like to change direction and get into non-profit," I said.

"Where do you think you'd like to work?" she asked.

I was still picking up low, female chatter from nearby offices that made for a congenial, warm atmosphere. "*This* is the kind of place I'd like to work," I said. "Any job openings here?"

"Actually, we're starting a new training program called Women Working Technical, and we could use someone to promote it and our other non-trad programs. But it's up to Rena, the director of the Center, and she's not here today. I'll give her a copy of your resumé. Call her and tell her I suggested you meet."

We talked some more about my background; she invited me to tour the rest of the Center. As we passed Laraine's office, I noticed a small lamp on her desk that cast a warm, rosy glow. *A nice homey touch,* I thought.

Denise introduced me to several counselors whose offices were in the back, and two others who shared a large open area on the opposite side of the office. I noticed a third desk was unoccupied. *Mine perhaps?*

Physically, the rooms were drab, but each counselor had added something to make her space more personal—a lamp here, a wall-hanging there. I wanted to be a part of it.

Before leaving, I stopped to say hello to Laraine. She said she really liked her work, that the women were great. I whispered that I was going to call Rena and hoped to work there. She whispered back, "Good luck."

I CALLED RENA THAT FRIDAY and met with her early the following week. Her office was through a door to the left of the seating area just inside the building's main entrance.

"How're you doing?" she asked—thin, fortyish, with a sharp nose and piercing eyes. She got up from her seat behind a large desk to shake my hand, motioned me to a chair, and sat down again. She gave me a quick smile that was soon replaced with a serious expression. Every inch of her desktop was covered with piles of papers, and stacks of publications took up a significant amount of floor space.

She searched through some papers on the desk. "I know Denise gave me a copy of your resumé, but I can't seem to find it."

"That's okay, I brought some copies with me." I handed one to her.

She quickly read it. "I see your last job was handling public relations for a packaging firm. Why did you leave?"

"I wanted to get into the non-profit field and help people more directly. Helping women get training in non-traditional fields appeals to me." I didn't mention that my previous employer was my mother.

Rena asked a few more questions and then told me she'd get back to me before the end of the week. I left her office not sure where I stood.

Two days later she offered me the job. I was ecstatic. For a non-profit, the salary was pretty good, and I'd be reporting to Denise. I needed to come in on Monday to fill out papers and begin work the following week. I called Laraine to tell her.

CHAPTER 33

OUR LOCAL POSTMAN DELIVERS OUR MAIL through a front door slot. It scatters over the rug in the foyer. When I come home from work, my first priority, after parking the car in the detached garage, entering the house through the side door, and putting my briefcase and pocketbook on the counter in the kitchen, is to collect the mail. I approach the task with great expectation, and I'm often disappointed. Most of the time, it's catalogs and junk. But one day in late September, I was elated to discover the first issue of the *National Sibling Newsletter*.

One of the attendees at the sibling-loss conference had told me she and others from the MO-KAN chapter of The Compassionate Friends were going to start a quarterly newsletter for bereaved siblings. I had added my name to the list of subscribers.

The newsletter was typed and copied on ten pages of white, legal-sized paper. It included poems and short essays by bereaved siblings—primarily young people—-from across the country.

I dropped the other mail on the kitchen counter and sat on the living room couch, eager to read the new publication. It was a strik-ing collection of heartfelt remembrances, and I couldn't put it down until I had read every entry. I was deeply affected by the intensity of the writers' pain and loss—as I had been by *Losing Someone You Love*. I found the collective depth of feeling incredibly moving. All had struggled to make sense of their loss and come to terms with it.

Some sibs regretted fights they'd had with their brother or sis-ter; others wondered if they could have done something to prevent the death. One bereaved sister said she hadn't been able to cry; an-other hadn't been able to stem her tears. All expressed an over-whelming love for their deceased sibling.

I was part of their community, and I cried over their losses and mine.

I also found, in the first issue, "A Letter to Brothers and Sisters," from a bereaved mom and dad. In a few short paragraphs, they addressed some of the nagging questions surviving siblings yearn to ask their parents: Is your love conditional, based on how I act or what I do? Are you constantly comparing me with my sibling who is no longer here? Would it hurt as much if I had died instead?

THIS MOTHER AND FATHER EXPLAINED that their love sometimes seems conditional because of *their* inability to express their real feelings. They stressed that parents are not the towers of strength they appear to be when something like this happens. In their grief, they may magnify the accomplishments of the child they lost and forget their faults, but that doesn't mean they love us any less. They sometimes appear to be contradictory, too, when they hover over us at times and withdraw at others—they have to learn to let go of the illusion that they can protect their children from all harm.

A couple of entries in the newsletter remained with me long after I had finished reading them. One, a poem called "Purple Eyes," was particularly moving. It had been written by someone named Quinn, whose sister, Adrienne, had been killed in a car crash two years before. Adrienne had been fifteen, and Quinn seventeen, at the time.

Quinn recalled that, early one morning, to persuade her younger sister to come with her to their pretend tree-boat next to a stream in the woods, she had promised Adrienne a surprise when they got there. She was not sure what that surprise would be. When they arrived, Quinn told Adrienne to dip a strand of her hair in the water, place it on her cheek, close her eyes, say, "Hocus-pocus," and count to three. "When you open your eyes, everything will be purple."

Quinn was amazed when her sister began telling her how beautiful everything looked with a purple tint. She went on and on, and Quinn smiled and said, "I told you so." She was stunned and bewildered. "But honestly, Adrienne, before we began our walk home, I looked into your eyes, and they really *did* look purple!"

It was one of the most touching tributes I'd read. I went into the kitchen, where Bob was peeling cucumbers. "You've got to stop what you're doing for a minute and listen to this."

I read the piece out loud. When I finished, I felt a lump in my chest, and he had tears in his eyes.

"You read me anything else," he said, "you'll have me blubbering over the sink." He grabbed a paper napkin and dabbed his eyes.

When Bob was touched by something, his eyes welled up, and sometimes tears flowed. The kids teased him about this, but I found it charming. A moving passage in a book, or a scene in a movie, often had the same effect.

I wanted to tell Quinn how moved I had been by her essay. I wrote to Tammy, one of the editors, to get her address. When I didn't hear from her, I sent a second letter. A couple of weeks later, I received a note from Tammy that included Quinn's home address. She apologized for not getting back to me sooner. She had moved and hadn't received my initial letter.

She'll enjoy hearing how much the poem touched you, wrote Tammy. *I'm sure there were hundreds of others felt the same.*

I wrote to Quinn how her remembrance had affected me, and that I, too, had lost my fifteen-year-old sister when I was seventeen.

She sent me a long reply. She was in college, and her mother had forwarded my letter to her. She was pleased I enjoyed what she had written and added that she kept a diary and wrote often to Adrienne. She said she was having a hard time. *It is wonderful that you have written to me because I really needed some thoughtfulness.*

Quinn said she had been feeling better and finally coming to terms with Adrienne's death when her cousin committed suicide. *It's bringing back the loss of Adrienne*, she wrote. *I'm back at the beginning, and this will be never-ending.*

Quinn asked me to tell her more about my sister (*if you are comfortable writing about her*). She described her feelings about Adrienne and asked if they were similar to mine. *Does the pain ever go away?* she wondered.

I told her about Ruth and how helpful it had been to attend the sibling-loss conference. *I buried my pain for many years*, I wrote her. *It's only recently that I've begun to deal with my feelings.*

Another very moving piece in the newsletter was a poem called "The Elephant in the Room," by Terry, a young man whose sister had died. In it, he pleads with his parents to talk about her. The last of the three verses was especially powerful:

Oh, please let's talk about the elephant in the room.
For if we talk about her death,
Perhaps we can talk about her life?
Can I say "Barbara" to you and not have you look away?
For if I cannot, then you are leaving me
Alone. . .
In a room. . .
With an elephant.

One of the most devastating entries I read was by Matt who had lost three brothers. Two had died as infants—one of SIDS, the other of pneumonia. The third had been killed at seventeen by a drunk driver.

Matt named his eldest son Nathan after his seventeen-year-old brother. He said he believed with all his heart that his dead brother would prefer to be associated with a warm-hearted and cheerful child full of life and great promise rather than the lifeless images his parents have in scrapbooks and on the wall.

CHAPTER 34

I WAS TRYING TO FALL ASLEEP the first night of the Weekend Grief Recovery Group I was attending. It had been sponsored by the Rothman-Cole Center for Sibling Loss. When sleep eluded me, I began a journal in which I expressed my frustration:

I can't get to sleep. Something inside is really wrong. I think I'm too overwhelmed.

The three-day experiential workshop was being held at a retreat center outside Chicago. I had flown to O'Hare earlier in the day, and a van from the center had transported me and two other attendees who had landed at about the same time.

Jerry Rothman was leading the group. He was assisted by three other well-qualified experts in experiential psychology: Fran Rothman (Jerry's then-wife) and Pam Miller—who both worked with Jerry—and Pierre Girouard, a therapist from Canada.

I had stayed in contact with Jerry and read a lot about his work. When I received the workshop flyer, I'd eagerly signed up and was looking forward to it. But late at night after the first day, I felt I had made a terrible mistake.

The retreat center was a simple, one-story building with a kitchen, dining room, and meeting rooms in the hub, and two wings that housed small, modest guest rooms. There was a grassy area and some trees in front, along with several wooden benches; in back were scattered bushes and trees, and a walkway led to the parking lot.

Inside the entrance sat a registration table. Fran, a thin, soft-spoken woman in her forties, was seated behind it. She greeted us warmly and handed us a packet of information. It included our room numbers and the weekend schedule. There were no room keys.

It was a little after four. She told us to settle in and come back at five for the introductory session, where we'd meet the other participants and discuss our goals and expectations.

My room was small and spartan: a single bed, an end table, a dresser, and a narrow, free-standing clothes rack with several hangers. A small window faced the back. There was a brown area rug on the floor; the walls were painted off-white and devoid of decoration. I was happy to see the room had its own bathroom.

It was March, still cold and blustery outside but warm inside. We had been told to bring comfortable clothes. I washed my face, brushed my teeth, and changed into a cotton turtleneck, loose-fitting slacks, and sneakers.

At five o'clock, we gathered in the main meeting room. There was plenty of space to comfortably accommodate all fourteen of us—ten participants and four leaders. For most of our activities, we'd be sitting in a circle, though a couple of exercises would require that we lie down.

My heart was pounding as I took a place in the circle with the other attendees—nine women and one man. We introduced ourselves and said why we had come. Although our ages ranged from the early twenties to mid-forties, we all felt we were stuck in the grieving process after losing a sibling, and wanted to reach a better place emotionally.

An hour later, we broke for dinner. We sat at two rectangular tables and, over chicken, roast potatoes, and string beans, learned more about each other. The leaders helped the conversation flow. Most attendees were from the Chicago area or from other towns in Illinois. But one woman had traveled from southern California, and another from Raleigh, North Carolina, and there was me.

After dinner, we reconvened in the meeting room for the first of several experiential activities. "Do you know what that means?" I had asked Dianne, one of my new acquaintances. She was at least fifteen years younger than I, but we had talked over dinner, and I liked her easy manner.

"I'm not sure. I think the exercises will help us better express our inner feelings."

"Find a comfortable space on the floor and stretch out on your back," Jerry began. We did. "Close your eyes and breathe deeply while you listen to the music. As you relax and breathe deeper, you'll begin to release a lot of feelings that are deep inside."

He told us we would progress through the exercise at our own pace and should not be disturbed if others began crying gently or sobbing. If we began to cry, one of the staff would come by to help.

We closed our eyes, and the music began—a mournful classical piece. One of the solo instruments was a cello, a favorite of mine. I began to breathe deeply, and as I did, I could begin to feel the music reach inside me.

After a few minutes, someone began to cry. It increased, and soon she was sobbing. I kept my eyes shut and heard footsteps moving to where she was and low words of comfort as she continued to sob. In time, others burst into tears. I continued to take deep breaths.

All of a sudden, I welled up and began crying uncontrollably. Swiftly, Fran was by my side. She took me in her arms and began rocking me back and forth while she whispered to me.

"I loved her s-so much," I stammered between sobs. "Why did she have to d-die?"

Fran stroked my hair and comforted me as if I were a little girl. "It's okay," she said. "Let yourself feel the pain." We rocked back and forth for some time. I trusted her, and I was able to let myself go.

When I had calmed down, I began to hear others in the room. One who had begun sobbing was a beautiful young woman in her early thirties who hadn't said much in the introductory meeting or at dinner. A patient of Pierre's, her twin brother had been killed in a car accident. She began wailing, and Pierre went over to hug her and rock her.

"We were so close, best friends," she sobbed. "I feel I've lost half of my body." Her voice was especially affecting. "I can't live without him!"

At that point, I opened my eyes. She was in a fetal position in Pierre's arms, still inconsolable. I grieved for her as well as for myself.

By the time the activity came to a close, I was a dishrag. I could hardly move, but I felt better. I was amazed how the music and deep breathing had had such an effect.

We slowly got up, returned to the circle, and talked about the experience. All of it was powerful, and I was ready for bed. But we weren't finished. Jerry gave out colored markers and construction paper and asked us to transfer our feelings to paper.

When we completed our drawings, we showed them to the others and talked about them.

At that moment, I became angry.

I should have gone to my room after the exercise, I thought. I didn't leave the meeting room, but I lay down in a corner, away from the group.

"Do you want me, or someone, to sit with you?" Fran asked.

"No."

The workshop ended at close to eleven. We said goodnight and went to our rooms.

Two hours later, I was wide awake in bed, unable to sleep. My heart was racing. *Help,* I wrote in my journal. *Where do I go from here?*

I tried again to get to sleep, without success. Finally, I got up. *I don't know if this workshop is right for me,* I wrote. *Maybe it's too much all at once.*

At four a.m., I woke Fran, whose room was next to mine.

"I'm so sorry I disturbed you," I said, "but I'm suffering from acute anxiety, and I can't sleep."

"The deep-breathing exercise brought up a lot of feelings, and you're having a hard time dealing with them," she answered in a calm, soothing voice. "I think you'll find that the next couple of exercises will ease the agitation you're feeling." I trusted her, and her words calmed me. I went back to bed and slept for a couple of hours.

IT WAS HARD TO BE WITH THE OTHERS at breakfast—juice, cold cereal, yogurt, a variety of pastries, and fruit. I didn't say much and wondered how I'd get through the day.

For the first activity, we were asked to find a partner. Dianne and I chose each other. We were instructed to give each other back massages. Although I was uncomfortable with the idea, I went along with it. It turned out to be enjoyable.

Following that, we were given markers and paper again and asked to express how we felt. I drew a spine with heat and light radiating from it. There were black clouds in the sky, but they were much smaller than the spine, and grass was growing below. I was feeling very positive and relaxed, and my picture reflected this. We showed our pictures to the group and interpreted them.

After a lunch of soup and salad or a sandwich, we returned to the meeting room and re-formed our circle. Jerry turned to me. "Would you like to try an experiment to let more feelings out?"

" . . . I guess so."

He and Fran opened a blanket and spread it in the middle of the floor.

"Lie down and reach your fingers and arms up to the sky with palms facing each other."

I followed his instructions.

"Who or what are you reaching for?"

" . . . I'm reaching for people."

"Would you like someone to hold you?"

"Yes, but I don't think anyone will want to. . . ." I began sobbing. Fran came over, hugged me tightly, and I hugged her back. Then others got up, surrounded me, and picked me up on the blanket. They rocked me back and forth, carried me to the side, and gently set me down. Then everyone hugged me. After a while only Dianne was holding me, and I was holding her. Someone covered both of us with another blanket, and we continued to hold each other.

"I can't believe it," I repeated over and over.

I asked her how she felt, and she said, "Fine."

We remained like that a long time. Eventually one of the leaders placed Dianne's head on my shoulder, put my arm around her, and tucked the blankets around us. I held her, and Dianne said, "We're very much alike."

"I have a daughter named Karen," I told her, "and if I had had another daughter instead of a son, I would have called her Diane."

"My sister's name is Karen," she said.

Later I helped rock each of the others in the blanket and hugged them. When the exercise was over, they gave us a break. I went to my room and took a nap.

AFTER DINNER WE TALKED about the experiential activity. I felt calm and content, a part of the group. I told this to the others and listened as they shared their feelings.

Pierre asked the others what they thought when I had lain down in the corner the night before.

"I thought she needed space," Dianne said.

"She looked very rigid when she was lying down," John added.

"You were stiff on your back, and no one felt you wanted them to come near you," said Pierre. "Your body language kept people away."

That was how I had lived my life, I realized. I judged people very quickly, often telling myself they didn't like me, and kept my distance. In my mind I accused some people of being stand-offish when *I* was the one who created the distance, feeling it was safer.

We were sitting in a circle in the same room we'd met over the last two days. The overhead lighting was subdued, as it had been the previous evening, the shades drawn the same way. Yet the atmosphere was warmer. It enveloped me like the blanket and fellow workshop attendees had earlier.

I was offered a comforting nectar, and I drank it. For the first time, I felt connected to others. I was able to approach them and let them reach out to me. I realized I could take the risk of being close and not feel devastated if they pushed me away. It was an amazing revelation, and another important turning point.

ON SUNDAY MORNING, the feeling of connection continued. There was a breakfast buffet, and classical music played in the background. We were one cohesive group, and I was an integral part of it. Soon we would leave to go our separate ways, but we pledged to keep in touch with each other.

Jerry told us he would send us an attendee address list, and an evaluation form to fill out and return. Before we said goodbye, we formed a circle and joined hands. A poignant rendition of the song "The Rose," made popular by Bette Midler, filled the air and surrounded us. The words, about love, reached my core.

CHAPTER 35

WHEN I RETURNED FROM CHICAGO, I was in high spirits. My mood matched the weather, almost balmy compared to cold, blustery Chicago. "How'd it go?" Bob asked when he picked me up at the airport.

"It was *so* good. I had a hard time at first, and I wanted to leave. But the workshop leaders were great. They encouraged me to stick with it, and I'm glad I did."

I was still in group therapy then, and when Wednesday evening rolled around, I told everyone what a remarkable experience it had been. I felt close to them, and I wanted to tell them what a positive effect it had had on me.

"I'm very happy for you," Jean said. While not an original group member, she had been coming for several years, and we were often simpatico. She was thin, well-groomed, and usually displayed a serious demeanor. However, she smiled in response to my good news; the others nodded in agreement.

I described the deep-breathing exercise that, along with carefully selected music, had helped unlock long-buried feelings. "I cried like a baby at one point, and I felt the pain like never before."

At the same time, I knew I had to shed more tears before I let Ruth go. I needed to cry a little longer for the sister I had lost, and then say goodbye.

For a couple of weeks, whenever I was home by myself, I put a somber piece of music in the cassette player—Rachmaninoff's "Concerto Number Two" was one of them—lay down on the couch, and sobbed.

I tried to get a copy of "The Legend of the Rose," sung by Winifred Lucas, that had been playing on the final morning of the weekend workshop. Jerry said he'd had it for a long time and gave me the name of the publisher. I tried to reach them without success. Finally, I settled on Bette Midler's version, "The Rose." I listened to it and felt uplifted by the music and its message about the endurance of love.

A couple of weeks later, I sensed it was time to go to the cemetery. Bob was the only person who knew. "Would you like me to come with you?"

"Thanks for offering, but I need to go myself."

It was an overcast, chilly day in early April. *Perfect weather for visiting Ruth's grave*, I thought.

I drove south on the Garden State Parkway with Bette Midler blasting through the car speakers. My tears were flowing.

At the workshop retreat, my sobs had released loneliness, pain, and anger I'd buried inside for almost thirty years. Now I was crying because it was time to say goodbye to my sister and embrace the life of love and possibility still available to me.

The last stanza of the song, which reminds us that love endures everything, really struck me.

AFTER THIRTY MILES ON THE HIGHWAY, I took the exit for the cemetery. I drove past several modern high-rise office buildings, under a railway bridge, and past single-family homes before reaching the gateless entrance. I recalled the resentment I had felt when I went there with my mother and father after Ruth died. Now I was happy I had a place I could visit in my own time and on my own terms.

I hadn't been to the cemetery since my grandmother's burial nine years before. Although she lived in Florida, she had wanted to be buried near Ruth. The plot my parents had purchased when Ruth died contained six graves, and Grandma's resting place was near the granddaughter she had lost. My father, who had died in 1971, was also buried there.

I parked in front of the office. It had gotten chilly; I zipped up my jacket and went in to get directions to the family plot. A friendly, middle-aged blond woman behind the counter opened a map and highlighted the route. It was close to the main entrance.

I returned to the car, drove the short distance, and parked under a tree next to the path.

I got out of the car again and looked around, relieved when I saw no other visitors. I slowly covered the short distance to the plot and gazed at it.

The cemetery could do a better job of upkeep, I thought, and immediately chuckled. My parents had spoken often about the upkeep when I visited with them so many years before—how the ivy covering was turning brown, or that it needed to be trimmed.

What goes around comes around. "I've become my

mother," I said aloud.

Three graves were occupied, and my mother would be buried next to my father. *What about the fifth and sixth? Mine and Bob's?*

I sank onto the concrete walk in front of Ruth's grave and touched the footstone. I felt tears coming down my cheeks. " . . . Hi, Ruth," I whispered, choking back those tears. "I need to talk to you. . . . I love you so much, and I miss you so much . . . but I need to say goodbye and get on with my life." I felt my heart pounding and was crying softly by then. "I'll always love you and remember you, as long as I live. . . ."

I sat there for a few minutes more. The light changed as the steel sky opened up for a moment, throwing watery light on the gravestone as the chill sank farther into me. Tears streaming down my face, I spoke to my grandmother. "I love you, Grandma, and miss you very much. . . ."

Then I addressed my father. "Daddy, I loved you so much, and I know you loved me. I wish we could have talked honestly when you were sick. I miss you, and I wish you could have known your grandchildren, and that they could have known you. . . ."

I had a water bottle with me, which I opened with shaking fingers. I took a sip. I remained in front of Ruth's grave for several more minutes. The wind was blowing lightly, and the sky was again steel gray.

Finally, I rose and picked up three small stones from the soil on the other side of the path. I placed one on each footstone to signify that a visitor had been there.

I went back to her grave. "Goodbye, sweet Ruth." I turned to the car and left.

CHAPTER 36

*I*T WAS A REAL TURNING POINT *in my life. I learned new skills in reaching out and giving to others.* That was a quote from my evaluation, and Jerry had included it on flyers for future workshops.

"Would you like to be our East Coast contact person?" he asked me in a phone conversation. "People may call for information about programs or want to talk to someone locally who lost a sibling growing up."

"That would be great."

Several people called or wrote. I told them about the workshop, listened to their stories, and told them mine.

One was Carol, a young woman in her twenties whose sister had been killed in a motorized scooter accident while on her honeymoon in Bermuda. Carol had suffered her grief in silence.

"My husband wants to start a family," she confessed, "but I'm terrified the child will die from an accident or illness."

"I know how you feel," I told her. "I'm overprotective of my kids too because I'm afraid something will happen to them. When you lose your sibling, you feel more vulnerable. But I've come to understand through counseling that I can't protect them by worrying."

We talked a number of times, and then I lost touch with her. One day, a birth announcement arrived with the following note:

Thanks ever so much for all your support . . . you made a difference in my life. I was deeply touched.

I also called the head of the local chapter of The Compassionate Friends. I told her I had attended the first sibling-loss conference in Kansas City, and I asked if the local chapter held meetings for bereaved siblings.

"No, we don't, but it's a good idea. Before we do that, would you like to speak at our next meeting about what it was like to lose your sister as a teenager?"

"I'd be happy to."

My upcoming appearance was promoted in the next newsletter:

> *Sisters and brothers also grieve for the one we lost, and because they may be young and not fully understand, they may carry their grief inside of them for many years. Judith Eichinger, now a mother of two children, realizes she never fully grieved for her younger sister. . . . We will begin our June meeting with her personal story, so that in the future we can be more supportive to our surviving children.*

We gathered in a meeting room on the lower level of a nearby mall. I was very nervous, not wanting to say anything to hurt or offend grieving parents.

The room was spartan, with thin wall-to-wall carpeting in a color similar to wheat. A long table stood along one wall underneath high transom windows; it was covered by a white plastic tablecloth and several plates of cookies, paper napkins, a coffee pot, and hot paper cups.

Twenty people, mostly women, sat in a semi-circle. They ranged in age from their early thirties to late fifties. When I entered the room, several were chatting with each other, but they stopped talking and turned toward me. I took a seat facing them.

I told them about my sister's death and how my parents had been overwhelmed by their grief. "I had no outlet for my feelings, and I was very lonely. I also felt angry and guilty."

I described how the National Sibling Conference and weekend experiential workshop had helped me connect with my feelings. "It was wonderful to be with other bereaved siblings who had *been* there. As a parent, I know I'd have a hard time reaching out to one of my children if anything happened to the other," I confided. "What's most important is that a relative or family friend listen to surviving siblings and comfort them."

Most of the audience was warm and attentive. However, I noticed one woman who, despite a bright yellow sweater that reminded me of sunshine, looked sad and dejected. It was obvious her mind was in another place. By then, I'd found that there are people who are trapped by their grief, not ready to connect.

At the end of my presentation, the chapter president stood up and asked how the group felt about my leading a sibling workshop for their kids. They agreed to try it at the next monthly meeting. They'd invite their middle- and high school-aged kids to come, and I'd meet with them in a nearby room.

MY MEETING WITH SIBLINGS wasn't a bust, but it wasn't a triumph. A few kids came, but they were not forthcoming. I realized quickly that I was out of my league. They needed a trained child psychologist with experience helping children express their feelings.

It didn't help either that their parents were down the hall. Neither I nor the kids were comfortable being in such close proximity. We talked, but only on a very superficial level, which was just as well—I wouldn't have been comfortable if our discussion had elicited strong emotional reactions.

EARLY IN 1989, JERRY ASKED ME to help publicize a Grief Recovery Workshop the Rothman-Cole Center was holding in the Spring—a year after the one I had attended. I wrote a letter to several daily newspapers about my experience at the prior workshop, and how it had impacted my life, that contained the following:

> *With the help of exceptionally skilled professionals, we were able to help ourselves and each other begin to come to terms with our loss,* I wrote. *At the time I lost my sister, there were no support groups available, and I lived with the hurt and anger—now known as unfinished grief—for a long time. The weekend in Chicago, along with individual and group therapy, helped me. I know I'm not alone. There are many other adults who experienced a close loss when they were growing up and didn't receive the necessary help at the time.*

I MAILED THE LETTERS and waited a week. When I didn't get a response, I made follow-up calls. One was to Lindy Washburn, the health reporter for the Record, the daily paper that serves Bergen County, which includes Teaneck. She picked up the phone.

"Hello, Ms. Washburn, I wonder if you received a letter I sent you last week about a sibling-loss workshop being held in Chicago?"

"I did," she said matter-of-factly, "and I passed it on to one of our staff writers. We'd like to do a feature on early sibling loss featuring your story, along with information on local support groups as well as the one in Chicago."

"I'd be happy to research what's available nearby."

"Good. The writer will be in touch with you." She said good-bye before I had a chance to ask who that would be.

I hung up the phone in disbelief. The *Record* wanted to feature me in a story on sibling loss! I was giddy with excitement and terrified by the thought of exposure. Was I ready to come out of the closet?

One of the paper's staff writers, Mary Amoroso, called me early the following week. "I'd like to set a date and time for an interview. Does this Friday around ten work for you?"

"Sure," I responded. My heart was pounding, and my palms got sweaty.

"I'll be there first, and a photographer will join us later in the morning. If you have some snapshots of you and your sister, we'll include them."

Suddenly, I was riding a train going very fast.

I spent the next few days working feverishly to gather information about local services available for bereaved siblings. I had begun a personal library of publications and media that dealt with sibling loss. One book I read several times was *Unspoken Grief*, by Dr. Helen Rosen, a psychologist and bereaved sibling who lived in New Jersey; the book was based on the results of a study she'd conducted on sibling grief when she was a professor at Rutgers. I called her and got her permission to give the writer her contact information.

The Center for Help in Time of Loss in Westwood, New Jersey, ran support groups for children whose parents or siblings had died. The group leader was Charles Lochner; I called him about the article, too. He was fine with me giving Mary his name and number.

He also told me about Rob Stevenson, a certified counselor in death education who taught the popular course "Contemporary Issues in Death Education" at River Dell High School. Rob also counseled children and adolescents who had lost siblings. It was another good referral I could give the writer.

MY FIRST DECISION FRIDAY MORNING was what to wear. I don't like to shop, so I tend to live in a few pieces of clothing each season. My favorite winter sweater was one I had ordered from a catalog several years before. It was loose fitting, with a dark gray collar and cuffs and patterns of lilac and other soft colors on the front and back. I felt good in it and wore it over a lilac cotton turtleneck. Gray wool slacks, dark gray knee-high socks, and black loafers completed the outfit.

I had butterflies in my stomach, and my mouth was dry. I'd never been interviewed before for a newspaper article, and I was nervous.

Mary rang the bell promptly at ten. She was a pretty, trim blond in her early thirties. "Hi, nice to meet you," she said, and gave me a warm smile and hearty handshake.

I invited her in and hung up her jacket in the hall closet. We walked through the living room into the kitchen. Mary put her briefcase on the six-foot round wooden table.

"This is a nice room," she commented. "I like the rust-colored ceramic tiles on the floor and the abstract wallpaper pattern."

"Thanks. Would you like a glass of water?"

"That would be good."

I filled two glasses from the tap and brought them to the table.

"Where would you like to talk?" I asked her.

"Kitchen's fine, if you're comfortable here."

It was a sunny day, and bright natural light from the east was falling through the partly open wooden blinds above the kitchen sink. We pulled two chairs away from the table. I sat down, and Mary turned her chair to face mine. She settled in it and took a pad and pen from her briefcase.

"What was the worst moment you remember about your sister's death?" I was shocked by that opening question, but I knew the answer, having relived it many times.

"It was the moment she died," I said, looking down at the floor. "She was in the hospital, and I knew things were really bad. One of my parents' friends asked if I wanted to go to the cafeteria for a soda. When I came back, my dad was standing in the door of Ruth's room, tears running down his face. 'She's gone,' he said.

"Rather than being together as a family when Ruth took her last breath, they sent me away. It was the loneliest, most painful moment of my life."

As I described it to Mary, I again felt the pain, loneliness, and anger. But by then, I knew my parents had been trying to protect me, not hurt me. "Thanks to therapy, the sibling-grief conference in Kansas City, and the loss workshop in Chicago, I've been able to move past a lot of anger to acceptance."

Mary asked me about Ruth's illness and how it had affected me growing up. "Looking back, I recognize I was depressed and worried most of the time. I buried those feelings and tried to have a normal life, but I often just went through the motions. I became very independent, and I didn't let anybody get close to me."

I told her about the periodic emergencies when Ruth had to be rushed to the hospital. "Looking back, I realize it was a miracle she lived as long as she did. My parents left no stone unturned to find a new treatment or therapy. They also gave her and our family as normal a life as possible. They were truly amazing."

I said this and, with a start, realized my mother and father *had been* truly amazing; if I had been the sick one, they would have done the same for me.

Mary asked me about my relationship with Ruth.

"We were very close. Sometimes I'd be jealous of all the attention she got, but most of the time we were allies, and we loved each other very much. Yet when she died, I was caught up in my parents' grief and didn't think about my own.

"I was very upset by the movie *Ordinary People*, about the disintegration of a family grieving for one of its two boys," I told her. "That was a turning point for me.

"But the first time I recognized my own pain was a few years ago when I mentioned to a woman I knew casually that I'd had a sister who had died.

"'That must have been very difficult for you,' she said. I said, 'Yes it was.' It was the first time anyone had recognized *my* loss."

I gave Mary information about the Rothman-Cole Center and local professionals who provided counseling for bereaved siblings. Then the doorbell rang.

"That might be Al," Mary said. We both stood up and walked to the door.

Al Paglione was a staff photographer for the paper. He was casually dressed and had a bag with photo equipment slung over his shoulder. We shook hands, and he and Mary greeted each other.

"Mind if I look around for the best place to take some photos?"

"That's fine."

I led him through the living room, dining room, kitchen, and small family room. After considering several options, he said he liked the corner of the dining room that had an antique wooden pendulum clock on the wall.

"If you don't mind, let's move the rocker from the living room to the right of the clock. Sit in it and put some pictures of you and your sister on your lap."

As I did that, he rummaged around in his bag and chose a camera and lens. "Now, hold up one of the photos and tell me about it." He snapped away while Mary looked on.

When he was finished, I looked at the clock. It was close to one. "Wow, I can't believe how much time's passed."

Mary said she'd gotten more than enough information from me and was going to speak to the other people I had told her about. She'd call if she had additional questions. Al thought he had enough photos.

"That's it?" I asked.

"That's it. I appreciate your openness and honesty. It's a

good story."

"When will it be published?" I asked her.

"In the next few weeks. I'll let you know."

We said goodbye, and I closed the door.

Still in disbelief, I moved the rocker back to the living room and slid the kitchen chairs underneath the table. It wouldn't be real until I saw the article in the paper. I hoped I hadn't opened Pandora's box.

CHAPTER 37

TWO WEEKS LATER, on a Thursday, Mary called me. "The article will be on the front page of Sunday's Better Living section."

"That was fast. Thanks for letting me know."

I was matter-of-fact on the phone, but after I hung up, my heart started racing. *This is it. There's no turning back. Soon my story will be out there for all to read.*

Over the next few days I tried to follow my usual routine, but it was hard. The anticipation was driving me crazy.

Bob usually fetches the paper early each Sunday morning. He brings it in and pulls out the sports section. But on that Sunday, I bounded out of bed at the crack of dawn, pulled on sweatpants over my pajamas, ran down the stairs, grabbed a jacket, and headed out the door. It was chilly, with the sun just beginning to make its way over the horizon. I picked up the paper from the front walk and hurried back inside. Bob was already in the kitchen.

"Come on, let's see it," he said as I struggled to pull it out of the plastic bag in which it had been delivered. After a bit of fumbling, I succeeded and separated the *Better Living* section from the rest of the paper. On page one lay a full-color photo of me sitting next to the clock, with snapshots of me and Ruth on my lap. The story took up the whole front page and continued onto page two. I skimmed the article and then reread it more slowly.

"Whaddya think?" asked Bob.

"It begins just before Ruth is rushed to the hospital and describes how my mother and father sent me to the cafeteria just before she died. My parents come off pretty harshly. Other than that, I think it's great." I handed it to him.

After reading it, he said, "You're right about the beginning being harsh, but it's well-written and includes some good quotes from the others they called. It's very informative."

Over the next few days, I had my fifteen minutes of fame. At the library, in the supermarket, around town, people stopped to tell me they'd read the article. Often they were people I knew, but some I didn't. A few offered their condolences; others said they hadn't been aware of the issue. Some people passed me on the street and did a double-take. They didn't say anything, but I suspected they were thinking, *I know her from someplace.*

I received a number of phone calls. I remember three in particular.

One was from Robbie, a friend when we were both single in New York City. As soon as I heard her voice, I immediately pictured the earnest gray eyes behind her steel-rimmed glasses and head of short, naturally curly black hair. She had always been a good listener. She had married a couple of years before I had and moved to a community near Teaneck. We had lost touch.

"I had no idea you'd had a sister who died. That must have been very hard." Her empathy was heartfelt, and we talked for quite a while. Despite our busy schedules, we managed to set up a dinner date. So the article brought us back together, and we've remained close friends.

I also got a call from Janet, who lived down the street. She was tall and lanky, with dark, deep-set eyes and a ready smile. Although she was my age, her three sons were adults. We knew each other casually.

"After reading your story, I realized why I got into such a funk when each of my boys turned twenty-one," she told me. "One of my sisters died suddenly from a virus at that age, and I never made the connection until now."

She said she still hadn't come to terms with her sister's death and wanted to know more about the experiential workshop I had attended in Chicago. We also discussed the possibility of organizing a support group in our area for those who had lost a sibling when they were young.

Then there was Becky, a pretty brunette who lived in the neighborhood. She was younger than I and had two little daughters. Whenever we ran into each other, she was very friendly though somewhat shy. "My brother died from an accidental gunshot wound when he was sixteen," she told me. "I never talk about it, but when I saw the article in the paper, I had to call you."

She told me how she still missed him and remained angry about his death.

"Would you be interested in being part of a support group on childhood sibling loss?" I asked.

"Yes," she responded without hesitation.

I WANTED TO SEND COPIES OF THE ARTICLE to members of my extended family but remained unhappy about how my parents had been portrayed. I called Harriet, my group therapist, to get her advice on how to handle it. She had read the article too and agreed it portrayed them harshly. "Why don't you rewrite the opening paragraphs the way you wished it had been written and send them along with the article?"

I thought that was an excellent idea. The newspaper had said my parents were in Ruth's room when I came home from a blind date and told me, "Go to bed." In my version, I made it clear that they were obviously very upset and had sent me to bed in an effort to protect me. (Later that night, an ambulance rushed Ruth to the hospital, where she died two days later.)

I sent the article and my revised opening to my relatives. I also called my two favorite aunts to thank them for their support when I was growing up.

JANET, BECKY, AND I STAYED IN TOUCH and talked more about forming a support group. We wanted to keep it small and have a professional lead it. We decided to ask social workers we knew for advice.

We hit a brick wall at first. Then I called a bereaved sibling who had gotten in touch with me several months earlier, and she suggested I call Dr. Sue Simring, a psychologist practicing in Englewood, New Jersey. Sue was very interested in facilitating our group and invited me to stop by her office the following afternoon.

Englewood is adjacent to Teaneck, so I didn't have far to travel. Sue's office was in a professional complex that looked like large, private homes. I stopped to read the directory to the right of the driveway. Most tenants were in the medical or mental health field.

Sue's building, at the far right corner, had a rustic look. It was a two-story house with weathered natural shingles. Four closely spaced, double-hung windows jutted out over the front door. They were framed in dark green, and the front and side doors were painted the same color.

I was most impressed with the foliage. Tall maples and firs stood on the near and far sides of the building, along with several bushes, including a large one on either side of the main entrance.

I parked the car in one of the spaces in front. Sue had instructed me to go to the side door and push the buzzer next to her name. When I did, she buzzed me in and ushered me into her first-floor office.

She was a slim, attractive woman—a few years younger than I—with a broad smile and shoulder-length, honey brown hair. She welcomed me and motioned for me to sit in the brown leather chair at the side of her desk. She settled into the larger one in front. To my right was a matching love seat and a dark wooden chair with a cushion.

"My mother lost her brother growing up," she said, "and she never got over it. It haunted her throughout her life. Facilitating your group will help me learn more about the effects of sibling loss." She said she would lead the six-week group free of charge. "One of my patients recently lost his brother in a car accident," she told me. "Would it be all right if I asked him to join us?"

"Absolutely," I said. His name was Gary.

WE BEGAN TWO WEEKS LATER. Janet, Becky, and I lived close enough to carpool. Gary, an earnest-looking young man in his early thirties, was already there when we arrived.

Sue got the ball rolling. "In my preparation for this group, I found that people rush to say goodbye to a loved one who's died but don't really say hello first. It might be good to say hello to our siblings before we say goodbye."

She asked us to respond to two questions: *What do you think your sibling liked about you, and What do you think your sibling would have liked about you today?*

"I remember a letter Ruth wrote to me at camp," I said. "She wished she could have been there with me and missed me. In that letter, and in her body language, it was obvious she looked up to me and admired me."

The others also responded with similarly positive memories.

"How can you take the things your sibling liked about you and incorporate them into your own life today?" Sue wanted to know.

"After Ruth's death, my parents," I said after a long silence, "particularly my mother, sometimes said I was cold and uncaring. But Ruth would have found me very caring." I choked up as I voiced this realization. "I can incorporate her positive feelings about me in my struggle to build self-esteem."

Becky said her brother would have appreciated her not being as shy, and Janet concluded her sister would have found her generally supportive. Gary said his brother would have backed his decision to leave the family business and go out on his own.

After our first session, I jotted down my feelings: *At first I wondered if the support group would really benefit me, since I've already done a lot of work. But when we started by saying hello to our siblings, I felt it was going to be very worthwhile for me and help me remember the positives.*

The other five sessions were also fruitful. During one of our meetings, I said, "I'd like my mother to acknowledge my loss. I'd like her to say, 'That must have been terrible for you.'"

"Are you willing to ask her directly for what you want?" Sue asked. "Tell her what you need from her, and if she doesn't or can't provide it, you may be able to stop looking for what you can't get."

It was great advice, but I never asked my mother that question. If I have any regrets, that's one of them.

Sue asked us again to think about how to incorporate into our everyday lives the positives our siblings saw in us.

"I know we were pals and companions," I replied. "I want to remember more of that."

My assignment after one of our sessions was to talk to people who had known me and my sister when we were growing up. "What was Ruth like as a person, and what were you like to-gether?" Sue asked.

We also talked about displaying family pictures. "I've always wanted to do that," I said. "It'll be a meaningful project for me."

At one of my regular group-therapy sessions with Harriet, I de-bated whether I should delve into the past again to try to remember the good times Ruth and I had had together. What would I gain?

My therapy group's recommendation was for me to stop trying and get on with my life. "There may not be that much to remem-ber," one person said.

"In time, when you're not trying, it'll come to you," said an-other. I wasn't sure what to do.

When I asked the sibling-support group the same question, my answer came from Gary. "It will help you smile when you think of her," he said.

I spoke to several of Ruth's friends and a cousin who had been closest to her in age. They all said she'd been a lot of fun.

I also made a lunch date with Mom to ask her how Ruth had felt about me and what she and I had liked to do for fun. We met at a bustling diner in downtown Millburn, across from the train station.

"She liked to do things with you," Mom said. "You used to draw pictures for her when she was sick and made things out of paper and cardboard. She looked up to you, admired you, wanted to do whatever you were doing. You both liked to go on family trips and plan what to see along the way."

We paused when the waitress brought our food. Mom savored her BLT (bacon very crisp) on rye toast, and I enjoyed a tuna salad on whole wheat. We ate silently for a few minutes. Then she continued, "You both made signs for special occasions and planned surprises for our birthdays and anniversary. You also played 'dress-up' a lot. You pulled down the steps to the attic and pretended to board a plane. You both loved to take car trips, and you'd play car games in the back seat. One favorite was who could spot the most license plates from different states."

As Mom spoke, I began to remember, too. "Ruth and I often played 'wedding' when we were young," I recalled. "We'd take turns putting on your long dressing gown and marching down a pretend aisle."

We reminisced for a long time. Gary had been right: The memories made both of us smile.

CHAPTER 38

URING THE YEARS I WAS actively dealing with the loss of my sister, I began reading any book about sibling loss I could lay my hands on. One of the first was the novel *At Risk*, by Alice Hoffman. In it, eleven-year-old Amanda contracts AIDS from a blood transfusion. The story focuses on how her family, friends, and neighbors deal with her illness and imminent death.

When I read it, my heart went out to Amanda's younger brother, Charlie. He's eight, and his mother and father aren't paying much attention to him. They are frantically trying instead to deal with Amanda's health crises and hospital visits. As her condition deteriorates, Charlie is shunted aside.

Before she is rushed to the hospital for the final time, she's in her room, battling a high fever. Her parents are in despair. Amanda's on her school's gymnastic team and couldn't attend a crucial competition the night before. The next morning, she asks Charlie to find out whether the team won. After school, Charlie wants to tell her, but as he's running up the stairs to her room, his father, Ivan, stops him.

> "*We don't want any noise up there,*" *he says.*
> "*I have to tell her something,*" *Charlie says.*
> "*It can wait,*" *Ivan says.*
> "*No, it can't,*" *Charlie insists.*

Ivan asks him what he has to tell her that's so important, and Charlie explains that she wants to know whether her team won.

> "*Well?*" *Ivan says.*
> "*Well, they did,*" *Charlie says. His face is hot and he feels as if he's going to cry. . . .*
> "*I'll tell her,*" *his father says. "*Do your home-work downstairs today.*"

My stomach churned as I read that—it was so reminiscent of the moments before my sister died.

When his parents and Amanda leave on what will be her final trip to the hospital, Charlie remains at home with his grandparents. He gets on his bike and heads towards the pond, near the marsh not far from his house. It's become his place of solace. He gets off the bike next to the pond and says to himself that, whenever asked, he'll always say he has one sister, Amanda. He'll never let himself forget her. *"Not in a million years."*

The Prince of Tides, by Pat Conroy, affected me deeply as well. Tom's twin sister has attempted suicide, and his older brother is dead, but the reader doesn't initially know the circumstances.

Slowly, the plot reveals the horrors that took place in the family home one night, and how emotionally damaged Tom and his siblings have been as a result. In therapy, Tom begins to remember the incident, and we discover with him why his sister was so intent on killing herself, and why his brother succeeded. His wrenching pain becomes ours, and his eventual catharsis is ours, too.

The fictional character who's haunted me the *most* through the years has been Holden Caulfield. I read *The Catcher in the Rye* in high school but didn't get what it was about.

But I picked it up again when I was researching sibling loss, and I knew immediately why Holden was acting the way he was. Anyone who's lost a brother or sister growing up recognizes that Holden is doing what he's doing, and saying what he's saying, because he's in extreme pain over the death of his beloved younger brother, Allie, who died of leukemia four years earlier.

Bereaved siblings feel Holden's pain after the first fifty pages. Yet most teachers and critics haven't a clue.

"I think the book is very overrated," said a member of my book club when it was mentioned at one of our meetings. At the time, I wasn't comfortable challenging her. To do so would have exposed my own vulnerability.

But for bereaved siblings, reading *Catcher* is an "aha" moment. In the first paragraph of her review in *The New York Times Book Review* of two young adult novels that deal with sibling loss, author Elizabeth DeVita-Raeburn writes the following: "When a friend in high school told me *The Catcher in the Rye* was the funniest book he'd ever read, I picked it up and sobbed my way through it. To my friend, Holden Caulfield was a hilarious smart aleck; to me, he was a bereft sibling, falling apart after his younger brother's death."

Elizabeth's older brother died of a rare immune deficiency syndrome when she was fourteen. She wrote about the impact of losing a sibling in her wonderful book, *The Empty Room: Understanding Sibling Loss.*

The online *Melrose Newsletter* is published monthly by a group of retirees in and around Melrose, Massachusetts. Several years ago, Ed Boyd, a psychologist who took up writing after retirement, did a piece for it entitled, "Revisiting *The Catcher in the Rye.*"

In it, Boyd expresses his amazement that, in all that's been written about Holden Caulfield, there is almost no mention of his brother's death. He cites an essay by Professor Edwin Haviland Miller, published in the Winter 1982 edition of *Mosaic* as one of the few exceptions. Miller writes: "I propose to read *Catcher in the Rye* as the chronicle of a four-year period in the life of an adolescent whose rebelliousness is the only means of dealing with his inability to come to terms with the death of his brother."

THROUGHOUT THE BOOK, I felt Holden's pain and despair. In a story he writes for his roommate Stradlater to submit to his composition teacher, Holden includes a wonderful description of Allie's baseball mitt. The piece then morphs into Holden talking about his kid brother in glowing terms and reveals that he died of leukemia. The night of his brother's death, Holden says he broke all the windows in the garage and would have broken the car windows, too, if he hadn't busted his fist. He says his fist still hurts once in a while, years later.

I felt his deep sorrow and got a big lump in my throat. He feels so lost and alone, and doesn't connect to the origin of these feelings.

Toward the end of the book, Holden has a conversation with

his little sister, Phoebe, after he's sneaked into the house. He's been kicked out of private school and is especially depressed.

In the course of their conversation, she expresses her disappointment about his expulsion. When he tells her all the things he didn't like about the place, Phoebe accuses him of never liking anything, which he denies. When she asks him if there's anything he *likes,* he says he likes Allie. When she points out that Allie's dead, he says he can still like someone after his death, "especially if they were a thousand times nicer than the people you know that's alive and all."

I have always felt that Holden yearns to be the catcher in the rye to save other children from his brother's fate.

At one point, I mentioned to Jerry Rothman that reading novels about sibling loss had given me great comfort. He asked if I could make a list of the books to post on the Center's website. I listed five works of fiction and two movies, along with brief descriptions of each. In addition to *At Risk, The Prince of Tides,* and *The Catcher in the Rye,* I included *The Deep End of the Ocean,* by Jacquelyn Mitchard, and *Invisible Circus,* by Jennifer Egan. The movies I mentioned were *Stand by Me* and, of course, *Ordinary People*—the film that began my quest to come to terms with the loss of my sister.

Several people thanked me for the suggestions and added other books to the list.

I also have read many non-fiction books about sibling loss. Each has provided me with additional knowledge and solace that I'm not alone.

CHAPTER 39

FAST FORWARD TO A BEAUTIFUL fall day in 2014. It was sunny and mild, perfect weather for the fortieth anniversary celebration of the kidney camp program. Mom had died five years earlier, just short of her ninety-sixth birthday. After her death, the foundation board voted me in as the new chair. When I took over, I had mixed feelings. It was hard work, and I resented having to devote so much time to it. But several years into the volunteer job, I'd come to view it as a gift from Mom.

"Running the foundation enables me to do something very rewarding for kids with kidney disease," I told Bob one evening over dinner. "I've gotten past the anger I felt when my parents founded it after Ruth died. I've been thrown into a leadership role, and I like the challenge."

"You're doing a great job," said my ever-supportive husband. Through the years, he'd also become involved with the foundation, designing our stationery, business cards, booklets, and more.

The fortieth-anniversary celebration featured folk singer-song-writer Lorre Wyatt. Even in high school, he had written poignant, meaningful songs. At graduation, which would have been Ruth's had she lived, he had written an especially beautiful song that he dedicated to her.

I had always described Lorre to others as a good friend of Ruth's. In truth, however, I knew better. He had confessed to me long before that he fell in love with Ruth the moment they met in kindergarten. They'd grown up together through elementary school, middle school, and the first year of high school until Ruth died. For my sister, it was a close friendship, but to Lorre it had always been much more.

Wayne Cabot, an anchor for WCBS News radio in New York City, served as master of ceremonies. He was a friend and former colleague of one of our board members. The program also included the current Millburn High School choral groups, the Millburnaires and Millburnettes. Lorre had been a Millburnaire, and several former members of the two groups from his and Ruth's class would do a couple of numbers with Lorre.

The foundation worked on the event for close to a year. It was held in the sanctuary of a synagogue in Millburn. Two weeks before the big day, I fretted to the co-chairs, "Less than a hundred people have bought advance tickets."

"Calm down," they both said. "Many people will buy them the day of the concert."

They were right. An hour before it began, there was a line out the door.

The sanctuary of the synagogue was warm and festive. The walls and pews were in varying shades of natural wood, and seating was in the round. Windows above the walls revealed a cloudless sky and let in beams of sunshine. The *bimah*, or platform, was decorated with fall fruits, vegetables, and foliage left over from the harvest festival of Sukkot, which had ended a few days before. Several steps below the *bimah* stood a lectern, covered by a velvet fabric. From there, the rabbi sometimes delivered his sermon or addressed the congregation.

The celebration was a huge success. Close to three hundred people came. The pews were filled, and a number of attendees sat on folding chairs the custodians had hastily set up behind the permanent seats. There were former classmates of mine and Ruth's, top staff from the camp and hospital, many friends and relatives, and Karen and Daniel and their families. Best of all, kidney campers and their parents came.

I knew ahead of time that the event would be packed with emotion. The confluence of remembering Ruth, Lorre's songs, my parents' legacy, and the presence of so many former classmates was a strong emotional mix. Growing up, I had never spoken to school friends about how terrified I had been that Ruth would die, and how I'd maintained a stoic exterior afterwards. At this event I was afraid that all these repressed feelings would tumble out.

I sat in a front pew between Frost Valley's chief executive officer and our web master, who was videotaping the event. Behind me was one of the pediatric nephrologists from the Children's Hospital at Montefiore in the Bronx—which provides medical oversight of the kidney camp program.

I looked around at the faces, some of which I hadn't seen in years, and was overwhelmed. They'd all come to celebrate with us and show their support. It was hard for me to take it all in. I felt light-headed and flushed. To get through it, I realized, I'd have to tamp down my feelings as much as possible.

Wayne Cabot was great. Tall and handsome, with a shock of sandy-colored hair and a smooth, deep voice——perfect for the radio——he connected immediately with the audience and lent humor and style to the event. He introduced me, and I stepped to the lectern. I welcomed everyone, thanked them for coming, and gave a tribute to my mother. It had been her revolutionary idea to have a kidney camp program where kids with kidney disorders could be mainstreamed with healthy campers. I reminded the audience that there was no other camp program like it in the world. I felt good standing before the audience in a black top with pink and purple patterns, a black skirt, and purple-and-silver earrings.

THEN WAYNE INTRODUCED LORRE, who approached the lectern guitar in hand. The last time I saw him had been twenty years earlier, when he was the sole performer at a folk concert in the area. At the time, his hair had begun to gray and he had gained some weight, but he'd still looked like the Lorre I knew in high school. He was wearing a gray T-shirt and khaki slacks, his hair thinner, and he was heavier, but he still had that signature smile and knew how to keep an audience engaged. When he began to sing, I was heartened to hear his voice was as clear and mellow as I remembered.

For the celebration, he'd written a special song about Ruth called "Like New Mown Hay." I knew my ability to keep my emotions intact would be tested when he sang it, because I was familiar with the lyrics. He'd sent them to me ahead of time. The words were deeply moving in their phrasing, lyrical quality, and depth of feeling.

It was about Ruth a time long ago. When he introduced the song, he spoke about her in wistful terms. Singing about her laugh, he stopped briefly, chuckled, and said he remembered her laugh well. At that moment, it became clear to everyone how much he had loved her.

During the song, Karen's nine- and ten-year-old daughters slipped out of their seats and sat on the floor in front of me. While their eyes stayed focused on Lorre, they leaned back against my legs. Daniel's four-year-old daughter followed suit. The girls' gesture, along with the song lyric, overwhelmed me, but I succeeded in keeping all of these intense feelings inside.

Then the high school choral groups sang, and they were marvelous. Lorre also sang some songs with several former classmates who had been choral members with him.

People from the camp and hospital, who partnered with the foundation, spoke, as well as a former kidney camper who had served in recent years as a counselor and activities director.

When the concert ended, everyone piled into the social hall to grab seats at one of the round tables covered in white tablecloths. On each sat a centerpiece of fresh fall flowers. Two large flower arrangements framed a rectangular buffet table, with generous platters of fruits and pastries.

Many who were there came up to me afterward to say hello and tell me how fabulous the concert had been. I was very happy to reconnect. A couple of former schoolmates whispered to me, "Did you know how Lorre felt about Ruth?"

"I had an idea."

After a while, he came to say goodbye. I thanked him profusely, and we hugged. He lived several hours away and had stayed with one of his former classmates the night before. He wanted to get a head start on his trip home.

During the next few days, many called or emailed to tell me what a great event it had been. "Take some time to bask in the glow of what you accomplished," one person said. I did, but after a week went by, the glow dimmed, and a malaise set in. I didn't know where it had come from and ignored it as much as possible.

Weeks went by. I went through the motions of daily living, but that *down* feeling persisted. I finally recognized it as mild depression. *How come?* I asked myself. *The concert was a smashing success. Why can't I enjoy the moment?*

I had terminated therapy a number of years before. There had no longer been a need. Now, I considered getting some professional help. But I had a gut feeling I could solve the problem myself if I could connect to the root cause.

Then one day I knew what it was. The concert had stirred up the profound loss I felt over Ruth's death. Yes, I had dealt with it years before, but the confluence of seeing Lorre again, hearing the song, seeing so many from long ago who had known Ruth, had been overwhelming. Once again I realized how deeply I had loved her and how angry I still was that she died.

I felt an urgency about what I had to do. The next day, I got into the car and drove to the cemetery.

As soon as I entered the grounds, I realized how much the cemetery had grown in a few short years. There was a whole new section to the left of where the family plot was located. Even the old section now stretched to the Garden State Parkway, where thousands of cars whizzed by every day. Years ago, there had been a buffer of trees and shrubs between the two, but no more.

That early December day, a cold, brisk wind was blowing from the west. Above was a solid gray sky. I didn't know what was going to happen, but I needed to visit my sister's grave.

I knew exactly where to go. I turned right onto the first narrow road between headstones, took the next right, and parked under a tree on the right-hand side. I zipped up my coat and wrapped my scarf around my neck as I climbed out of the car. I hurried up the cement path to the plot and gazed at the graves of my mother, father, sister, and grandmother. *I'll have to speak to the office about my mother's grave,* I thought. *We pay for perpetual care, and half the ground cover is dead.*

I sat down in front of Ruth's footstone and didn't say anything for a while. It was quiet, except for the rustle of leaves. Then I began to speak. "Ruth, we had a great concert a few weeks ago. Lorre sang such a poignant song about you. He loved you so much. So many of your friends were there. You would have loved it. But you weren't there, and it made me so sad." I began to cry.

I reached into the depth of my being as I continued. "I loved you *so* much, and I miss you *so* much," I sobbed. "As long as I'm alive, I will always love you."

I cried until there were no more tears left.

Then I paraphrased what eight-year-old Charlie had said about his dying sister, Amanda, at the end of the book, *At Risk*: "Whatever happens, I'll always have a sister named Ruth. And when my children and grandchildren ask me, I'll tell them everything about you. . . . I'll never forget you, not in a million years."

A weight had been lifted. I stood up, gathered four small stones, put one on each grave, and headed back to the car.

ACKNOWLEDGMENTS

Thank you, Barry Sheinkopf, director of The Writing Center in Englewood Cliffs, New Jersey, for being a terrific editor and providing the guidance and encouragement I needed to write this book. I am also grateful to the members of the Tuesday morning writing seminar who gave me much-needed support and shared their stories. Thanks also to Christopher Woo for his help with cover production, and to Chris Chaberski for his excellent proofreading skills. A special thank-you as well to Bob Ghiradella for recommending Barry and Chris.

Thank you, Lorre Wyatt, for sharing with me your music, memories, and love for Ruth.

Thanks to Dr. Jerry Rothman, director of The Rothman-Cole Center for Sibling Loss in Chicago (now The Center for Grief Recovery and Therapeutic Services), whose experiential weekend workshop provided a turning point in my life. He was also a friend and died too young. Thanks to my individual therapist, Nohmie Myers, and group therapist, Harriet Copeland—along with group members—for helping me make the journey from grief and anger to acceptance. Harriet died several years ago, and I miss her.

Thank you, Dr. Sue Simring, for facilitating the six-week sibling loss support group that enabled me to remember the fun times with Ruth. I am also grateful to the other members of the support group, who provided me with suggestions and clarity.

I salute my parents, Eva and Ira Gottscho, who chose to live productive and meaningful lives helping others with kidney disorders after suffering the most difficult of losses, the death of a beloved child.

Thanks to my children, Karen and Daniel, for their love and support. And most of all, I thank my husband, Bob Eichinger, who is always there for me and is a graphic designer extraordinaire (he designed the book's cover). I could not imagine traveling life's journey without him.

JUDY EICHINGER

ABOUT THE AUTHOR

Judy Eichinger received her B.A. from Penn State and spent much of her professional career as a writer of corporate and non-profit communications. She also facilitated job readiness workshops at the Bergen One-Stop Career Center in Hackensack, New Jersey. She currently serves as board chair of The Ruth Gottscho Kidney Foundation and lives with her husband, Bob Eichinger, in Northern New Jersey.

CPSIA information can be obtained
at www.ICGtesting.com
Printed in the USA
BVOW08s0443020418
512141BV00002B/5/P